GREEN

—

Simple Ideas for
Small Outdoor Spaces

Ula Maria

Photography by Jason Ingram

MITCHELL BEAZLEY

Contents

Introduction
SMALL IS BEAUTIFUL

———

It was only after moving into an apartment on a busy London street that I really began to appreciate the summers of my childhood spent in a large country garden, watering tomatoes and picking cherries. A small outdoor space is a treasure, and whether it's a front garden, a minuscule courtyard or a petite roof terrace, it can be transformed into an outdoor room full of life and personality. The generous urban garden with a sweeping manicured lawn has become something of a rarity, so the way in which we curate our small outdoor spaces has become all the more important. Fortunately, small needn't mean lifeless or dull. Given enough consideration, even the tiniest of outdoor spaces can result in the most creative and imaginative gardens.

There is a general misconception that an attractive garden equals a green-fingered owner, but don't let this discourage you from creating the garden of your dreams. You don't have to be a plant guru to have a beautiful and functional outdoor space. There are styles and types of gardens to suit every individual. This book is an invitation to revisit your outdoor space and discover gardening opportunities where you least expect them. It is packed with ideas and inspirational outdoor spaces, ranging from a tiny 5 sq m (54 sq ft) productive balcony to a contemporary front garden that doubles up as an outdoor room, proving that no space is ever too small or insignificant to be something of beauty. Start small and the chances are that the more time you spend outdoors, the more you will fall in love with gardening.

Although often ignored, small gardens have many advantages that suit the lifestyles of city dwellers. Our busy schedules and long working hours mean there is often little time for tending our gardens and subsequently even less time for enjoying them, so the smaller the space, the easier it is to transform it. A limited budget will go further and have much more impact in a small space than it would in a large

garden, simply with the introduction of statement plants and sculptural furniture.

Stepping outside the comfort zone of your home into the unknown of the outdoors might seem daunting at first, but remember that, unlike interior spaces, even the best gardens are never truly finished and are often frayed around the edges – and that's the beauty of nature. This book is a guide to unlocking the potential of small outdoor spaces, helping you to discover your ideal garden style and showing you how to create it. In return, you will experience the joy of creating an outdoor space that you truly care for.

APPROACH

There are so many possible ways of approaching the design of an outdoor space that it may be hard to know where to begin. It always helps me to think of a garden as an extension of the home, an outdoor room full of potential, with spaces for play, dining, resting, and, above all, reconnecting with nature. A garden will always work best if it ties in well with your lifestyle, the amount of time you like to spend outdoors, and the kind of activities you are interested in. It is important to keep reminding yourself that, unlike architecture or interior design, a garden is constantly evolving. It doesn't have to be perfect from the outset, and there is always room for improvement at a later stage.

ABOVE Draw inspiration for your outdoor space from the interior design of your home, using complementary or contrasting materials, colours and other design elements. **OPPOSITE** Consider the views from inside your home, and think of windows and doors as picture frames to be filled with the most beautiful living displays.

Begin by identifying how you would like to use your outdoor space. The more practical and functional it is, the more encouraged you will be to use, tend and care for it.

If your lifestyle doesn't allow you to spend much time outdoors, concentrate on creating beautiful views through the windows that you look out of the most. They will make a huge impact on how you feel.

First impressions count, so don't forget about your front garden, regardless of its size. It is a miniature representation of what can be expected from the rest of your home and, inevitably, its owners. After all, it is the front garden that greets you and your visitors first.

It is important to assess your surroundings, not only to give your outdoor space a wider context, but also to distinguish the key aesthetic factors that brought you to live there in the first place. On most occasions, you will be able to take inspiration from the vernacular architecture and the landscape. For example, if the dominant materials of the architecture are timber, brick or concrete, the materials for your garden can be chosen to either match, complement or contrast with their colour and textural qualities.

SCALE

—

One of the most common questions asked when working with a
small urban garden is how to make it appear bigger. This is a tricky
task that requires careful consideration of scale and proportion, and
an understanding of how each one of the design elements relates to
their setting, and to each other, and, most importantly, to the human
scale. It is made even more challenging by the fact that, unlike
interior spaces, gardens are living and ever-changing. As a result,
the scale of the garden varies over time, too. Plants grow taller than
anticipated; they self-seed and outgrow spaces. Mastering the art
of scale requires time and it is often a case of trial and error, but I
believe that the key to success when working with scale in small
spaces is to think big and be imaginative!

ABOVE A sense of place in the tiniest of spaces depends hugely on
beautifully crafted details, where every nook and cranny counts.
OPPOSITE Specimen plants, furniture and other elements become
focal points throughout the garden, intriguing the eye, creating a
journey and distracting from the overall small size of the space.

There is a temptation to fill a small space with small
elements, such as small paving units and plants.
However, this often results in a garden that appears,
well, small. Although it might seem counterintuitive
to have large plants and objects in a small garden,
if chosen well, they can make a space feel larger.

Introduce plants of varied height and texture into
your beds and planters, to create interest and depth
and the illusion of a larger space. Identify your key
structural plants and work your way down in scale
from there.

It is important to have a range of items of different
sizes in your garden that will still work well together
as a whole. Introduce some super-sized planters,
sculptural light fittings or furniture and scatter
them throughout the space, then use some smaller
design elements and furnishings to link them all
together. This way, the attention will be focused
on all the beautiful individual items and not the
size of the overall space.

Identify what you would like to use as the focal
point of the space, to draw the eye and create a
journey through it. This should be the largest
object in your garden, perhaps a set of furniture,
a sculpture or a specimen plant.

COLOUR

—

Colour is without doubt one of the most crucial design considerations in a garden, helping to determine the mood of the whole space, whether it be exciting, calming, inviting, energetic or subdued. It is a powerful tool that can change how the whole garden is perceived. One of the most common mistakes made by enthusiastic gardeners is overdoing the variety and mixture of colourful plants, which often results in an indistinct garden. For those who are yet to master the use of colour, following the rule of "less is more" is essential.

ABOVE The most obvious way of introducing colour is with flowers, but in small spaces, where the choice of plants is limited, foliage can provide longer-lasting and equally effective results.
OPPOSITE Colour has a huge effect on the overall atmosphere of a space and should be carefully considered for all the design elements.

To achieve unity within a planting, look to nature for inspiration. Remember how magical the carpets of bluebells in the woods look in spring, or the swathes of white cow parsley in the countryside. Try to find a group of plants that grow and work as well together as these prime examples in nature.

You can also begin by picking two or three of your favourite colours. For the most part, these should be complementary, rather than clashing, to ensure they work well together. Once you have chosen the plants, place them in large groups and swathes, adapting and distilling the inspiration from nature.

You may choose to introduce colour into your garden through hardscape materials such as paving, small structures, fences or garden furniture. In this case, neutral and simple planting is most likely to work best.

Most of us were introduced to the colour wheel at school. For those who are less experimental, it can provide a strong starting point for some classic, fault-proof colour combinations, whether you are after neutral, contrasting, complementary or analogous schemes.

TEXTURE

Texture can have a huge impact on the way an outdoor space
looks and feels but, unfortunately, it is often an overlooked design
consideration. Above all, it can affect the overall atmosphere of
a space visually, and it never fails to amaze me how different the
same material can look when given a different finish, whether it's
timber, stone or concrete. Texture can also make a space feel larger
or smaller, brighter or darker, contemporary or rustic. It can even
influence the way we move through a space. Likewise with planting,
the textural qualities of plants provide interest all year round, unlike
the fleeting appearance of flowers alone.

OPPOSITE The most fascinating planting schemes are often the
result of a clever use of texture. Whether smooth, glossy or matte,
the contrasting textures of foliage and stems are bound to turn into
a rich, year-round plant tapestry. ABOVE Different paving textures
can be used to distinguish the separate uses of specific areas.

Different textures will affect the overall style and
aesthetic of an outdoor space. Smooth textures,
such as polished concrete or sawn stone, are often
used to create a slick, contemporary look, while
tumbled setts or weathered timber will likely result
in a characterful and aged atmosphere.

Use contrasting textured surfaces to differentiate
the functionality of the various areas and influence
movement through the space. Rough, uneven
textured paving could be used to slow down traffic
and demarcate thresholds, while smooth and even
surfaces encourage comfortable movement.

Plants rich in texture can create intriguing and
captivating planting schemes that don't rely on
flowering periods or seasonality alone. Consider
using foliage in a variety of different textures,
from very coarse and rough to smooth and silky.

Contrasting textures can be used to introduce
richness, depth and interest in even the smallest
of spaces. The texture of key structural plants
can be used to influence the palette of hardscape
materials and vice versa. Although texture should
be considered for each individual item, it is most
important not to forget how the different textures
will come together and coexist in one space.

MATERIALS

—

Planting naturally plays a crucial role in a garden, but it's important not to forget that it is the hardscape that forms the bones of every outdoor space. Our journey and experience of the garden are often determined by the quality of the materials used to create pathways, patios, steps and boundaries. Unless a hardscape element is designed to be a focal point of the garden, I believe the best practice is to begin with a subtle base, which you can then build on by introducing layers of personality over time.

ABOVE Timeless, neutral materials should form the foundation of the garden, which can be enriched with characterful design elements and details over time. **OPPOSITE** In highly constricted gardens where little will grow, distinctive materials can transform the space from dark and abandoned to the most striking feature of your home.

Small, enclosed spaces tend to allow for more adventurous material choices. Being more forgiving because they are isolated from their surroundings and wider context, they offer greater freedom when exploring which style of outdoor space to choose.

The diversity of materials and their treatments that are available can be quite overwhelming if you are creating a garden from scratch. Think of your garden as another room and consider materials you have used inside your home. Repeating materials used indoors on the outside works incredibly well in small spaces. In most cases, you will be able to draw inspiration from the existing features, whether these are the bricks of the house or a wooden floor.

Select timeless-looking materials for permanent garden features, such as patios, decking or walls, that form the backdrop for more temporary elements like furniture. This way, you will be able to manipulate the atmosphere of the space without breaking the bank through major reconstruction.

The simpler and more refined the material palette, the more cohesive the garden will look. Visualize your hard-landscaping material palette as a pictorial background for your garden. The plants will then become the true stars of the painting.

Style

Unruly Haven

ULA MARIA

I created this chic and secluded haven out of a small urban back garden measuring just under 30 sq m (323 sq ft). Beautiful, chaotic nature has been packed into every conceivable nook and cranny, to make up for the lack of space. The design is contemporary and rich in personality, with earthy materials, such as clay pavers and weathered timber, contrasting with the abundant planting. The layout of the garden is based on strong architectural forms being reclaimed by nature. Sun-bleached grasses nestling under fig trees have been left to grow as tall and unruly as they wish. Wild strawberries, sage and dill thrive among them, blurring the boundaries between a kitchen garden and a meadow-style planting. At the end of the garden is a vintage table for outdoor dining, its solid appearance making it a focal point in the garden.

OPPOSITE The garden path is framed with *Euphorbia mellifera* on one side and a gnarled fig tree on the other. At the end of the vista is a Tibetan cherry (*Prunus serrula*), with its copper-coloured bark.

RIGHT Filled with ornamental grasses, salvias and perennial plants, the garden border softens the appearance of the contemporary wooden fence.

Untamed Contemporary

• Think of creative ways of reclaiming and incorporating existing materials found on site. In this case, old railway sleepers (ties) form a characterful raised bed at the back of the garden, giving extra height to the three Tibetan cherry (*Prunus serrula*) trees used to provide privacy.

• Think about the views you wish to have from inside the house and how they will change over time. Large plants in the foreground will partially obscure the view, creating intrigue and adding a sense of depth.

• Undulating lines aren't necessary to achieve a naturalistic look. In a contemporary design, allow plants to break boundaries and overgrow hard edges.

• Earthy materials like clay pavers and timber add warmth and charm, and age beautifully over time. Consider the various material finishes available to help achieve a different look and feel.

• Most grasses are easy to care for and look brilliant all year round. They also create movement and soften hard edges, such as paths.

ABOVE LEFT Fig trees make beautiful feature plants with their gnarled branches, large exotic foliage and fruits that turn deep purple when ripe. **ABOVE MIDDLE** Clay pavers and timber radiate warmth and authenticity. **ABOVE RIGHT** Soft *Stipa tenuissima* grasses are interplanted with jewel-like flowering plants such as *Potentilla thurberi* 'Monarch's Velvet'.

OPPOSITE Vintage pots and planters in various materials are scattered throughout the garden, bringing a layer of interest and soul to this newly built space.

"I sought to create a space that would have a soul and character but wouldn't feel like a pastiche. This garden is an ever-evolving relationship between strong architectural forms and nature breaking their boundaries."

ULA MARIA

THIS PAGE The raised bed at the back of the garden has been created out of reclaimed wooden railway sleepers (ties) found on site and doubles up as a bench alongside the dining table.

Colours of the Desert

MARTHA KREMPEL

———

Enclosed yet accessible from all four sides, this courtyard is a celebration of outdoor living, with spaces to unwind, entertain or simply escape the hustle and bustle of the city. "The palette for the garden is the colours of the desert, the bright green and blue-greys of the desert foliage set among the often pink rocks, dusty ground and desert flowers," explains garden designer Martha Krempel. The design for the garden was inspired by a family trip along Horseshoe Bend River in Arizona. Shades of grey dominate the hard surfaces of the garden, seamlessly uniting a variety of spaces into a single courtyard. The concrete floor is enriched by the material and texture of the inset clay pavers, which complement the bricks used for both the inside and outside of the house. This combination of concrete and brick creates a surface that is both contemporary and characterful. The unassuming colour is subtle enough to act as a backdrop, allowing the planting to take centre stage. Outdoor living is embraced by giving over a part of the garden to a large dining table, perfect for family gatherings or entertaining guests, while the sculptural fireplace with its built-in log storage radiates cosiness and warmth – an idyllic setup for sitting around the fire with loved ones and making many more memories.

OPPOSITE ABOVE The planting starts inside the house with a mature candelabra tree (*Euphorbia ingens*) in a bed of grasses, connecting the interior with the outdoor space.

OPPOSITE BELOW A mix of seating provides opportunities for alfresco dining, relaxation and sitting in front of the fire.

"In 2015 my family and I toured, in a circular route, the four states of Arizona, Nevada, Utah and California, taking in Antelope Canyon, sleeping overnight in the Mojave Desert and driving through majestic landscapes. It was an incredible experience, and Horseshoe Bend River became a metaphor for our journey. I have imposed my version of that river on the garden to link the doorways and entrance points in it, creating places to stop and sit and take in the sun."

MARTHA KREMPEL

Family Time

• A prominent fireplace becomes one of the garden's focal points. It is also the perfect place to spend an evening with family and friends, no matter what the season, as well as quietly reading a book and escaping the noise of the city.

• Create a seasonal biodiverse green roof to absorb rainwater, attract wildlife and help to improve the polluted urban air. There are so many types of green roofs to choose from that there's one for even the trickiest of sites.

• Contrasting hardscape materials help to differentiate various garden areas. Smooth concrete surfaces shape the paths, while textural carpets of clay pavers denote more restful parts of the garden, such as the dining area and space around the fireplace.

• A large *Euphorbia ingens*, commonly known as the candelabra tree or cowboy cactus, has been planted indoors against the garden window panels. Surrounded by grasses, it truly blurs the boundary between inside and out, merging them into one large living space.

ABOVE Log storage is incorporated into the design of the sculptural fireplace, creating a practical as well as aesthetically pleasing feature.

ABOVE The biodiverse green roof of the owner's home provides a striking display of seasonally changing planting patterns that can be viewed from above.

ABOVE As well as providing textural interest, the grey brick paving laid in a stretcher bond is used to denote specific areas within the garden.

ABOVE Splashes of pink planting are dotted around the garden, reflecting the desert-inspired colour scheme. **LEFT** A striking fireplace is one of the garden's key features, with the large, weathered wooden beam adding character and grandeur.

OPPOSITE The contrasting shapes and sizes of trees and shrubs create intricate shadows that flicker on the muted grey paving on sunny days. **ABOVE** With the interior garden a continuation of the courtyard space, the lush tropical and desert-inspired planting can be enjoyed all year round. **LEFT** The linear forms of clay paving are reflected in the beautifully crafted wooden furniture, creating a unified design language.

Garden of Contrasts

GEORGIA LINDSAY

—

Large courtyard gardens in the middle of a city have become
something of a rare luxury. Yet, walking along the streets of a
city, it becomes obvious how many front gardens are underused,
being either overgrown or covered in gravel. This 42 sq m
(452 sq ft) front garden, designed by Georgia Lindsay, proves that
they shouldn't be ignored. Running the width of the property, this
joyful, multifunctional garden doubles as a car parking space when
required. The bifold doors of the house open up directly onto the
seating area, where there's a built-in bench filled with cushions
– it feels as if the interior space is spilling out into the front garden.
Large, corten-steel panels resemble pieces of abstract art.
The porcelain paving is laid in two-tone stripes across the
width of the garden, to make it feel bigger.

OPPOSITE From the paving to the planting and
accessories, every single item in the garden has
been carefully selected to complement the blue
and orange colour palette.

ABOVE A magnolia tree has been planted to poke
through the built-in wooden bench. One day it will
envelop the seating area with its large-leaved canopy.

Orange and Blue

• The classic contrasting colour combination of orange and blue dominates this courtyard. Contrasting colours appear on opposite sides of the colour wheel, with orange and blue, yellow and purple, and red and green being the most powerful.

• Shades of orange are used, not only throughout the hardscape and furniture but in the planting, too. Rust-accented plants include *Coprosma repens* PACIFIC NIGHT, *Euphorbia griffithii* 'Fireglow', *Euphorbia amygdaloides* 'Purpurea', *Heuchera* and *Anemanthele lessoniana*.

• Porcelain paving in contrasting tones of grey complements the linear architecture of the building. It has been laid in stripes perpendicular to the house, and in varying widths, to accentuate the width of the courtyard.

• Custom-made, corten-steel panels with an abstract leaf design enclose the space, providing a unique theatrical backdrop to the garden. In the evening, light spills through the scored parts, creating drama. This ensures the space is welcoming and exciting all year round without relying on plants to breathe life into it.

ABOVE Discreet light fittings on the wall appear to blend into the design of the garden gate without detracting from the subtle warmth of the light they produce.

ABOVE The surface texture of the custom-made, corten-steel panels echoes the shapes of the magnolia leaves, creating playful shadows when the sun shines.

"The corten panels form the main focal point, giving a sense of mystery as to what lies beyond. This is vital in a small space, to avoid feeling hemmed in. At night they transform the space magically with dappled shadows and pools of light cast from the rear. The laser-cut shapes were inspired by the large rounded leaves of the evergreen *Magnolia grandiflora* 'Kay Parris' that emerges from the L-shaped bench. The rounded shape of the leaves is also echoed in the large Scottish pebbles, which form a circle beneath the tree."

GEORGIA LINDSAY

LEFT The planting palette is dominated by rust-accented foliage that complements the overall colour scheme. **TOP** Contemporary café-style furniture provides flexibility without limiting the small space. The woven seat and lattice table results in pieces that look both elegant and playful. **ABOVE** Large and showy white magnolia flowers provide a theatrical seasonal display.

City Wildflowers

BUTTER WAKEFIELD

Filled with scent and texture, garden designer Butter Wakefield's city garden radiates a dreamy countryside feel. There's a carpet of wildflowers at the centre, providing seasonal interest for people and wildlife. Purple and pink flowers dance in the breeze, introducing movement to the otherwise formal lawn. Yew (*Taxus baccata*) pyramids provide structure, creating rhythm and continuity throughout the space. Typically associated with large-scale landscape gardens, they sit just as comfortably here, bringing a sense of grandeur to an enclosed space. Every corner of the garden is filled with containers, from stone and terracotta planters to tiny metal pots, yet they all speak the same language. With the colour palette of the plants beautifully refined and cohesive, it is the layers of texture and form that create depth and blur boundaries.

OPPOSITE ABOVE This garden was unloved and neglected when its present owners moved in, consisting of just a shabby lawn and scruffy shrubs. But there were two promising trees – an apple and a magnolia. **OPPOSITE BELOW** A cosy seating area is nestled under a large magnolia, which provides shelter and shade. **RIGHT** The romantic, countryside-inspired planting includes wildflowers and herbs, mostly in shades of pink, white and purple, and topiary shrub specimens.

Countryside in the City

- You can bring the feel of the countryside to the smallest of spaces by filling planters, windowsills and every patch of ground with an abundance of foxgloves, herbs, roses and wildflowers.

- Topiary specimens provide structure, form and winter interest. Place them to frame views, define areas or introduce rhythm and grandeur.

- Creating a carpet of wildflowers is not as challenging as you might think. There are even companies that supply wildflower turf, which will give an instant effect with minimum effort. The installation process is almost as simple as rolling out a carpet.

- The seating area is nestled under a striking magnolia tree adjacent to the house. Its large trunk is decorated with fairy lights, a playful touch that lights up the space at night.

- Turn an awkwardly shaped corner into a workstation with a potting table covered in pots, urns and planters. You can even hang an old mirror for a touch of quirky charm.

ABOVE The garden is filled with planters for growing herbs and flowers, from large antique urns to tiny terracotta pots and vintage metal cans.

ABOVE Topiary specimens are repeated throughout the garden alongside the lawn, giving a rhythm and year-round structure to the space.

ABOVE Taking centre stage in this garden is a carpet of softly coloured purple and pink wildflowers, which makes the lawn appear less informal.

RIGHT AND FAR RIGHT Soft pastel shades of pink and blue flowers – red campion (*Silene dioica*) and *Campanula poscharskyana* 'Garden Star' – are dotted throughout the garden, giving a traditional countryside feel.

BELOW The style and colour palette of the garden are a true reflection of the owner's home and perfectly complement the decorative details, such as this specially commissioned painting by artist Sarah Bowman. Sarah is renowned for her landscapes framed by windowsills.

> "My own garden, with its simple layout and design, is a source of great joy and provides me with a great sense of wellbeing, and my home with a much-needed green emphasis."
> BUTTER WAKEFIELD

OPPOSITE A charming workstation with dozens of pots in a corner of the garden is dedicated to potting and propagating plants. **LEFT** A rustic steel obelisk reminiscent of a bird cage supports tall plants and provides sculptural interest. **TOP** Interwoven stems form a ball reminiscent of a bird's nest. Hanging from a branch, it makes a charming accessory that could double up as a light fitting. **ABOVE** A rich profusion of flowers overspill the edges of large antique urn enveloping it in green foliage.

A Hidden Retreat
ADOLFO HARRISON

—

Contemporary yet characterful is a difficult trick to pull off, but garden designer Adolfo Harrison proves that it's a challenge worth taking. This garden exhibits an exceptional play of light and shadow, colour and form. Every view of it is completely different, yet there's an undeniable unity and a distinct atmosphere throughout. The large pinnate leaves of the stag's horn sumach trees (*Rhus typhina*) turn rich orange in autumn, a reflection of the burnt orange walls of the property, Western Red Cedar cladding and corten-steel planters. Most of the plants, including an Indian bean tree (*Catalpa bignonioides*) and the sumachs, are planted in pots, providing extra height and sculptural form. The distressed metal chairs, with peeling paintwork, are a charming addition, suggesting the garden has been there for a long time, aged by the weather over the seasons.

OPPOSITE The dusky apricot-coloured garden wall injects warmth into the enclosed courtyard and provides a distinctive backdrop for the plants.

ABOVE The atmosphere on the upper terrace is luscious and tropical, with the broad canopies of trees providing shelter from the sun.

Soulful and Earthy

- The colours of the garden are shades of the earth: rusty oranges, muted browns, warm clay and cool greys. The containers, from large planters to the smallest of pots, are in an array of browns. Combined with the timber decking and cladding, they radiate warmth.

- The corten-steel planters create a powerful and distinctive atmosphere on the upper terrace. Luscious clumps of Japanese forest grass (*Hakonechloa macra*) spill over their edges, providing interest at mid-level, while *Rhus typhina* trees create theatre with their sculptural forms.

- The planting, in varying shades of green, is luscious and exotic. It includes an Indian bean tree (*Catalpa bignonioides*), sweet box (*Sarcococca confusa*), *Asarum europaeum*, *Euphorbia martini* and fig (*Ficus carica*) – all high-impact plants and relatively easy to look after.

- The courtyard floor is covered in silver-grey granite. Long rectangular flagstones form jagged-edge paths, while the remaining areas are filled in with small-diameter gravel. Interplanted with creeping ground-cover plants, they create a unique mat of contrasting patches.

ABOVE Vintage green metal chairs bring an industrial charm to the courtyard, with their patches of peeled-off paint adding a layer of texture.

ABOVE Plants like this hart's tongue fern (*Asplenium scolopendrium*) nestle into apparently inaccessible corners, just as they would do in their natural habitat.

ABOVE The stems of plants, which are often overlooked during plant selection, provide the most fascinating display of colour tones in this garden.

"By linking the separate courtyard and terrace with the staircase, we were able to create a circular flow between the exterior and interior spaces on both floors, while still keeping the atmospheres of both levels quite distinct."

ADOLFO HARRISON

LEFT Large, corten-steel planters of ornamental *Hakonechloa macra* grasses, their luscious foliage spilling over the top, dominate the upper terrace. **BELOW** The courtyard floor is a play of hard and soft surfaces, resembling a distorted chequerboard, with mind-your-own-business (*Soleirolia soleirolii*) creeping through the granite flagstones to form soft cushions of foliage. **OVERLEAF** This small courtyard is full of contrasting textures, from smooth and glossy to gritty and matte, resulting in a rich and visually stimulating space.

Balcony Garden
ALICE VINCENT

What could you possibly grow on a balcony that's just over
5 sq m (54 sq ft) in size? Well, if you ask author and self-taught
gardener Alice Vincent, her answer might take you by surprise.
Throughout the year, you can find lupins, tulips, hellebores,
camellias, anemones and many more seasonal plants on her
plant-packed balcony. Besides being in the middle of the city and
12 m (40 ft) up from the ground, it has become the most popular
wildlife attraction in the area, with multiple daily visits from squirrels
looking for seasonal bulbs. Often it is our fears and presumptions
that stop us from turning the smallest of outdoor spaces into
a green haven, but no space is too small – pots can be stacked,
planters hung from above and clipped onto walls, not to mention
trellis and other green wall systems.

"People with gardens think the balcony
is small, or constricting, but I know
how lucky I am to be able to look
after it. For me, life is out here – the
smell of the air when it rains, bees
on petals. Whatever is happening in
my day, the balcony will calm me
down, lift me up and offer me a
moment of pause that is often all
too rare in the rest of this city."

ALICE VINCENT

OPPOSITE A small balcony forms
a link between Alice's apartment
and the enormous trees just
outside the property, which provide
the most stunning green backdrop.
RIGHT Running around the outside of
the balcony is a long linear planter,
enlarging the constricted outdoor
space with an edging of plants.

Tiny Sanctuary

- It's a common misperception that nothing much can be achieved with a small outdoor space, but this needn't be the case. A small space such as a balcony forces you to be more creative in your planting. With less upkeep, it also means that you have more time simply to enjoy it.

- Seasonal plants can make all the difference in a tiny space. There are so many plants to be enjoyed in every season, from spring bulbs that light up the garden with a promise of warmer days to come to late-flowering dahlias, indicating that autumn is just around the corner.

- Make the most of every vertical surface. Attach hanging planters to railings, and plant trailing plants such as nasturtiums. Fix planters or trellis to balcony screening to create green walls.

- Although a balcony garden might not have the space for large areas of planting or hefty pieces of furniture, there's nothing to stop you from accessorizing the space with beautiful tools and furnishings. High-quality tools will encourage you to use them, and so spend more time outdoors and enjoy the little space you have to its full potential.

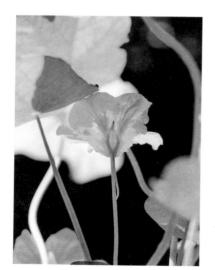

ABOVE Sun-loving nasturtium (*Tropaeolum majus*) trail over the edge of the balcony, enlivening the space with their bright orange and yellow flowers.

ABOVE Plants are stacked up on the floor at each end of the balcony, providing height. The layers of greenery form a cloud of textural foliage.

OPPOSITE There are plants everywhere on this balcony, and it's no wonder that some of its most regular visitors include bees, butterflies and squirrels.

New Naturalism
ADOLFO HARRISON

—

Some of the most successful town gardens are those where it is hard to define at which point the house ends and the garden begins. This spectacular city courtyard by garden designer Adolfo Harrison is proof of that. This is a contrasting yet sensitive combination of old and new, sharp and soft, crafted and naturalistic. The brick wall covered with moss and climbers is one of the original garden features that Adolfo has seamlessly incorporated into the new design. Garden paths float above slightly sunken beds filled with naturalistic planting. It all looks effortless, as if some plants have self-seeded and become interplanted with some striking specimens over time. A corten-steel water feature adds another dimension to the space. The sound of rippling water creates a sense of calm and attracts wildlife, transforming an urban space into a sensory oasis.

OPPOSITE A narrow timber path, set just above the flowerbeds, provides a link to the seating area. The entrance is defined by the tall wooden pergola, covered in luscious green foliage.
RIGHT Every garden should suit the lifestyle of its owners. The centrepiece of this section of the garden is the dining area, with a large built-in sofa on two sides.

Blurring the Boundaries

———

• Narrow down your selection of plant species to no more than ten. Plant them in large blocks or swathes for greater impact. Consider seasonal interest so there's always something to look forward to.

• Multistemmed trees introduce mid-height interest and form to a space. They often look more dramatic and characterful than single-stemmed trees due to their gnarled branches and interesting shapes.

• Using the same floor material for the house and garden blurs the boundary between inside and out. If the material is unsuitable outside, you can achieve a similar effect through colour, pattern or texture.

• The trickle of water can be both soothing and a powerful tool to drown out traffic noise. The simple rectangular shape embraces the contemporary design while the corten steel enriches it with personality.

• If entertaining friends and family is important to you, dedicate a generous part of the garden to a large dining table and invest in comfortable seating and atmospheric lighting.

ABOVE A variety of multistemmed trees and shrubs form clouds of green foliage in the summer, leaving gnarled and exposed stems to be enjoyed in winter.

ABOVE *Asplenium scolopendrium* ferns with their green tongues are dotted throughout the garden, creating a sense of plants that have self-seeded over time. **OPPOSITE** The transition between indoors and outdoors is seamless, with matching floor tiles and indoor planting that includes creeping fig (*Ficus pumila*), devil's ivy (*Epipremnum Aureum*) and *Philodendron xanadu*.

"The client wanted the atmosphere of the garden to remind her of the Barcelona courtyards of her youth. We concluded that the universal traits of these gardens that could be translated here are a well-worn and warm material palette, the play of light and shadows, plants growing in exposed cracks and climbing towards the light, outdoor living and the sound of water. In order to make the garden feel larger and more dynamic, we created a circular flow to the garden through the three seating areas, three trees and three corten-steel elements, providing multiple focal points that continuously lead the eye around."

ADOLFO HARRISON

Soft clouds of green foliage from multistemmed trees obscure the garden boundary, creating the illusion that it is a larger space than it actually is. OPPOSITE Dozens of *Iris* 'Action Front', a tall bearded iris, appear in spring to form a striking colour block of dusky burgundy speckled with yellow.

TOP A discreet water feature, nestled among the planting, waits to be discovered. Its surface of water glimmering in the sun is a soothing spectacle. ABOVE A collection of beautifully coloured and textured succulents in a shallow planter provides a long-lasting display. LEFT Introducing cosy and comfortable nooks for seating and alfresco dining encourages longer hours spent outdoors.

A Touch of the Mediterranean

MIRIA HARRIS

—

Designer Miria Harris has craftily turned an empty patch of land in central London into a Mediterranean-style dream. The dusky pink rendered walls, deep terracotta tones and vibrant furniture evoke a warm climate and outdoor living. A clay tile floor extends seamlessly from indoors to the garden, providing continuity and embracing the sense of place. The multicoloured tones and imperfections of the clay give the impression of a floor that has been there longer than the rest of the garden. Iconic planters by Willy Guhl inject the space with charm and personality, while charismatic black and white tiles by Bert & May form a feature wall reminiscent of a giant abstract painting. Mostly green-coloured plants balance these strong materials and soften the look, while birch trees provide dappled shade, movement and lightness.

OPPOSITE ABOVE Two distinct materials have been used to cover the courtyard floor: burgundy brick slips closest to the house and poured concrete leading to the garden studio. **OPPOSITE BELOW** Wispy silver birch trees and the shrub planting soften the angular lines of the hardscape. **RIGHT** Burgundy brick slips also appear in the central courtyard, where they contrast with the black-and-white geometric tiles used to create a striking feature wall.

Warm Terracotta to Dusky Pink

———

• Making the most of vertical surfaces where the space is highly constrained can transform that space from lifeless to incredibly exciting. Create extraordinary abstract art walls using graphic tiles that range in colour and pattern. This treatment will work particularly well when all the space you have is a light well, and there is not enough room for growing plants.

• Unique pieces of furniture can double up as sculptural elements, to inject a space with quirky charm.

• Pink isn't the usual colour that comes to mind when thinking about garden walls and floors, but here it is an inseparable part of the design. The colour palette of this garden is a play of terracotta hues, from dark ginger tiles to dusky pink-painted walls. It is a light-hearted choice that evokes the Mediterranean.

• A built-in outdoor kitchen area is the perfect way to embrace outdoor living. It is also the perfect excuse for hosting garden parties with family and friends.

ABOVE Standing out as a sculptural statement piece, this white Roly-Poly chair with its soft curves glimmers in the sun, highlighting the fun and charming design.

ABOVE Pink colour tones appear not only throughout the courtyard's hard surfaces but the planting, too. Here, pink fronds untangle themselves from the green fern cloud.

ABOVE This multifunctional built-in water pool, clad in the brick slips seen elsewhere in the garden, is both a children's paddling pool and an ornamental water feature.

TOP Rendered walls in a subtle pink bring out the warm colour tones of the wide-board cedar fencing. Both surfaces create a delightful backdrop for the vivid green planting. **ABOVE** An outdoor kitchen consists of a simple charcoal grill, sink and storage, providing all the essentials for outdoor entertaining and dining. **LEFT** A German beer hall-style trellis table and benches, positioned at the far end of the garden, are shaded by one of the silver birch trees.

OPPOSITE Creating the most striking outdoor space doesn't mean you always have to include an abundance of plants. Cleverly positioned graphic tiles can result in the most fascinating display. **LEFT** Iconic Willy Guhl planters help to introduce a burst of unexpected colour into the courtyard. They also blur the boundary between inside and out. **TOP AND ABOVE** Foliage can provide just as much colour as flowering plants. It is also likely to last far longer than seasonal blooms. **OVERLEAF** A simple yet powerful planting palette becomes far more intricate when viewed close up. It is always exciting to incorporate small details into a design, to be discovered over time.

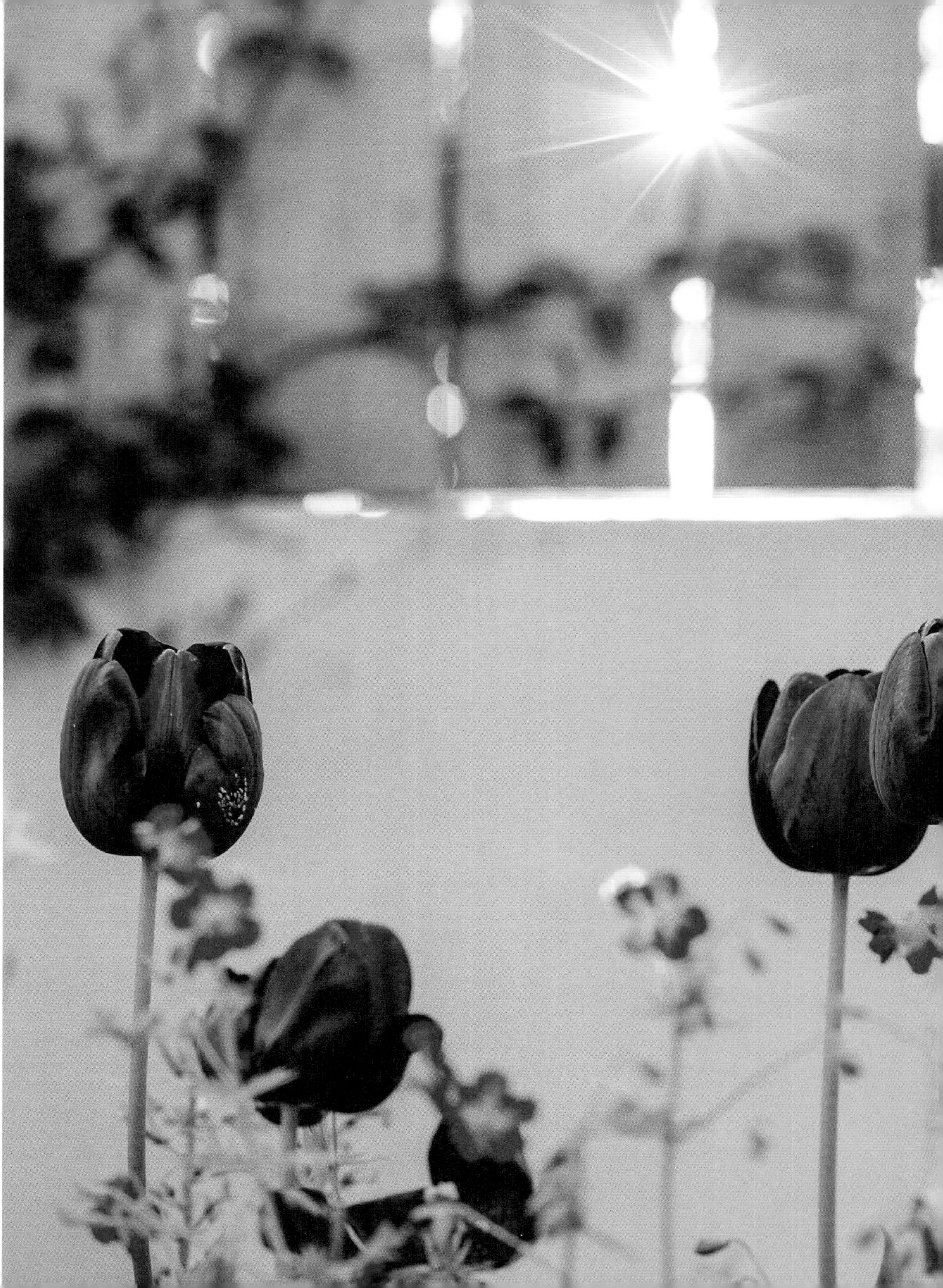

Romantic Idyll
PHOEBE DICKINSON

—

As soon as you open the large navy doors onto this fairy-tale-like garden, your lungs are filled with the hypnotic fragrance of roses. Artist Phoebe Dickinson, recognized as one of the most gifted classical painters of this century, has expertly assembled this garden layer by layer. Her garden has a painterly quality and is living proof that a newly created space can look and feel as if it has always been there. Antique furniture, sculptures and planters blur the boundaries of the garden, creating the illusion of a much grander space. Pale pink climbing roses envelop the wall in an abundance of showy flowers. Along with a variety of other climbers, they make the most of the vertical garden elements without compromising on floor space. A selection of quirky antique furniture that looks as if it could belong in a Victorian dining room is the focal point of the garden, seamlessly linking the interior to the outdoors.

OPPOSITE Stone carvings, antique furniture and vintage pots obscure every corner of the garden, transforming it into a mystical and enchanting world.

ABOVE When the large navy doors are left wide open the garden becomes a natural extension of the living room.

Classical Style

- Always keep an eye out for antique garden ornaments, which will result in a more personal and unique garden.

- Create original pieces of furniture by sourcing individual parts from different places. The base of the table is from an antique shop, while the top was made from a marble remnant at a stone specialist's yard.

- Candles in metal lanterns and carved stone holders are scattered around the garden, creating a soothing ambience. The candlelight is mimicked by discreet light fittings nestled among the plants.

- Inspiration for your garden can come from almost anywhere. This garden is inspired by the incredible collections of antiquities, stone carvings and furniture at Sir John Soane's Museum in London.

- It is no surprise that most antique items will have a hefty price tag, but don't be disheartened. Many of the items for this garden were found on eBay. Some cast-stone makers will also be able to supply hand-crafted pieces that closely resemble natural antique stone.

ABOVE The garden walls are decorated with characterful and unique stone carvings, most of which were found in various antique shops and on eBay.

ABOVE The colour palette is mostly soft and subtle, with pastel pink and purple blooms nestling among the green foliage like garden jewels.

ABOVE In a quintessentially English garden style, glorious pale pink roses clamber over the walls, adding to the fairy-tale appeal of this romantic idyll.

ABOVE LEFT The abundance of pots, planters and ornaments creates an intriguing display. No two are the same and each one is as fascinating as the next. **LEFT** There's nothing quite as enchanting as candlelight outdoors. Lanterns of all shapes, sizes and materials are dotted throughout the garden. **ABOVE** The table and chairs sit comfortably outside, suggesting that furniture designed primarily for the home shouldn't be overlooked when it comes to furnishing your garden.

PAGE 72 An old mirror hanging on the back wall is enveloped by climbing plants. As well as appearing to enlarge the small garden, it creates a fairy-tale-like atmosphere. **PAGE 73** Some of the more contemporary metal planters have been filled with ivy, which spills over their edges, softening the hard lines.

Lavender Hues

MARLENE FAO

—

A small and enclosed garden may seem a challenge but it definitely has its advantages. Unlike a large garden set in a wider landscape, an inward-focused space means you don't really have to worry about what happens outside its walls. When "My Mindful Home" blog founder Marlene Fao and partner moved into their home, the garden was a neglected grey box with mismatched, worn-out timber boundaries. They have slowly rebuilt the garden themselves by painting the fences and adding a built-in raised bed and furniture. Marlene used soft shades of lavender, white and clay to cover the decking and walls, evoking a Mediterranean beach house. The Mediterranean-style planting includes olive trees, lavender, rosemary, curry plant and mint. The garden's focal point is a large sofa with soft lilac pillows – perfect for relaxing and unwinding.

OPPOSITE Outdoor rugs have become quite a trend in recent years. Best suited to small city gardens, they really help to blur the boundary between indoors and out.

ABOVE The garden was an empty, gloomy and unloved space when its new owners moved in, but it wasn't long before shades of grey had been replaced with soothing lavender hues.

Mediterranean Vibe

• Select plants that embrace the style and feel of the garden you are trying to create. Studying nature or a particular landscape you are drawn to can be a great source of inspiration. The Mediterranean feel of this garden is evoked by the use of lavender, thyme, rosemary and olive trees – a true celebration of the garigue landscape of France.

• Invest in key pieces of furniture that will be used on a regular basis. There's no better way to unwind from the hustle and bustle of the city than spending an afternoon daydreaming on a large, comfortable garden sofa while soaking up the sunshine.

• Painting surfaces in a single colour or two closely related colour tones blurs the boundaries of the garden, making it feel bigger. This works especially well if you have a variety of boundary treatments neighbouring your garden but want to achieve a more unified look.

• Style your garden with furniture that will make the space feel more cosy. A drinks trolley (cart), an outdoor rug or a candle lantern will inject the garden with personality without breaking the bank.

ABOVE Drinks trolleys (carts) and trays make stylish additions to the garden, ideal for displaying potted plants as well as serving drinks on hot summer days.

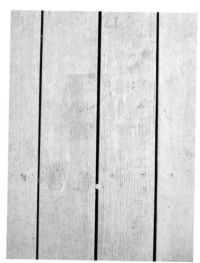

ABOVE The original garden decking has been rejuvenated with a whitewash stain, evoking the Mediterranean beach house vibe.

ABOVE The subtle warmth of candles and lanterns can be used to create the most enchanting atmosphere for a cosy summer evening in the garden.

"This DIY garden was designed to be low maintenance and functional – a peaceful, Mediterranean-inspired, small garden. I love the smell of lavender, rosemary and the olive trees, together with the calmness of the *Stipa* grass in the wind. We measured the garden a few times to make sure the furniture and flowerbed would fit nicely with the space. The raised bed was made by us with oak timbers. We then painted the fences, the flowerbed and the old decking. We did it all by ourselves and – for a first garden – we are really proud of it!"

MARLENE FAO

ABOVE A long and narrow built-in raised bed contains a display of Mediterranean plants, including robust and reliable olive trees, lavender and rosemary. **RIGHT** Marlene installed a custom-built steel wire grid to cover the back fence of the garden that she hopes will eventually become overgrown with climbing plants.

"The roof terrace garden sits on top of the owner's textile design studio. She longed for a space that would reflect both her inherent love of plants, but also her interest in the gardens of Russian dacha homes. Her garden is not only home to an array of perennial ornamental plants (some of which are found in her signature prints), but also a productive space with perennial crops. Marrow and courgettes [zucchini] can be found thriving next to dahlias and runner beans entwined with passion flowers."

GABRIELLE SHAY

Style

Floral Tapestry

GABRIELLE SHAY AND SILKA RITTSON-THOMAS

—

It is as if an intricate tapestry of plants has come alive and covered two-thirds of this city roof terrace with extraordinary blooms and foliage. In Gabrielle Shay and Silka Rittson-Thomas's design, the abundant naturalistic planting, mixed with jewel-like flowers and vegetables, overflows every hard edge and boundary. One of the biggest surprises is the garden's unpredictability – the way plants respond to the ever-changing seasons, the weather and their location. That's the beauty of a seasonal planting scheme, which becomes even more special when it's in an urban setting like this and the unruly nature of the plants provides such contrast. Being able to see nature undergo a full life cycle in one year is quite exciting and, as this garden suggests, nothing should hold you back from creating a full-blown ornamental meadow on your own small rooftop terrace.

OPPOSITE The tiny roof terrace garden is almost completely enveloped by plants, providing a green escape in the middle of the city.

ABOVE Wispy grasses and perennial plants create an awe-inspiring boundary between the terrace and street below, blocking out noise and creating privacy.

Exuberant and Romantic

- Although this roof terrace is small, its planting is tall and incredibly immersive. In many gardens, planters are often far larger than their plants, outweighing them in scale and proportion, but here the focus is completely on the plants. You would have to try really hard to see what they are growing in.

- The beauty of this garden is that there are plants everywhere, which lifts the space to another level. Narrow and awkward corners are often overlooked but here they are fitted with trellises of climbing plants.

- This compact interpretation of a Russian dacha – a small countryside cottage with a productive vegetable and flower garden – showcases how a rich tapestry of flowers and edible plants can be achieved in the most unlikely of places. The planting includes dahlias, dill, grapevines, runner beans and even some larger vegetables such as courgettes (zucchini) and squash.

- When an outdoor space is so small, the choice of furniture becomes even more important as it is such an integral part of the space.

ABOVE A tiny urban roof terrace can be just as effective for growing edible plants and herbs and welcoming wildlife, as an allotment.

ABOVE White bistro-style chairs and a table covered in a striking tablecloth inject a burst of the owner's personality into the space.

ABOVE Climbing plants are perfect for covering awkward spaces and vertical surfaces in foliage and pretty blossom.

RIGHT Showy flowers in deep colours such as this *Salvia* 'Love and Wishes' stand out against the naturalistic planting and create a rich floral tapestry. **BELOW LEFT** Sweet peas (*Lathyrus odoratus*) nestled among the grasses fill the air with a delicious scent. Their fragile flowers are reminiscent of colourful butterflies fluttering in the sun. **BELOW RIGHT** The terrace is planted with a rich variety of colourful and fragrant plants that attract bees, butterflies and various other insects, providing them with an important urban habitat.

Pared-down Modern
MIRIA HARRIS

———

Splashes of vibrant perennial planting stand out against the cool greys in this pared-down design for a modernist house by Miria Harris. Everything seems artfully balanced and no object demands considerably more attention than another. The predominant shape of the design is a rectangle, which can be seen in the layout, paving, seating, furniture and even the fencing. This repetition creates a strong design language. A variety of climbing plants covers the fence in a shield of green foliage. Providing dappled shade, a multistemmed silver birch (*Betula pendula*) overarches the seating area. The limited selection of objects in the garden makes it feel more spacious than it actually is. The choice of furniture in such a simple space is very important, because it is visible at all times from various points of the garden as well as from inside the house.

OPPOSITE A large, multistemmed silver birch, planted in the far corner of the garden, raises the sightline and enhances the small space visually.
RIGHT Tall, custom-made raised beds, which have been painted grey, help to create privacy and divide the garden into different areas.

Modernist Vibe

- The restrained colour palette of the garden – mostly shades of grey and natural wood, with white and black accents – complements the aesthetics of the modernist house.

- The garden floor is made of Staffordshire blue bricks and dark grey limestone slabs. The colours of the two materials transition seamlessly from one to the other, while introducing textural interest. Bricks laid on their edge and perpendicular to the house elongate the space.

- Custom-made raised beds painted grey match the overall colour scheme of the garden. They indicate the entrance to the garden and offer privacy from visitors at the gate. A garden bench, which doubles up as storage, has been created by fitting a wooden top to a planter.

- A multistemmed silver birch provides height and envelops the small garden in a subtle shield of green.

- Perennial plants in mostly pastel purples and pinks are dotted here and there, providing just enough colour without overpowering the space.

ABOVE *Aquilegia vulgaris* var. *stellata* 'Black Barlow' punctuate the otherwise calm colour palette of the garden with their deep sultry blooms.

ABOVE Staffordshire blue bricks, which have been laid on their edge to emphasize their slim rectangular silhouette, help to make the garden appear longer.

ABOVE Festoon lights add a touch of informality and provide a warm subtle light. They are easy to install and just as easy to move around without permanent fixing.

RIGHT Modernist aesthetics are also reflected in the garden furniture, which consists of Luxembourg style metal chairs, a wood and metal table, and a pair of white Hay Hee lounge chairs. **BELOW** A built-in bench with a wooden top doubles up as storage space – the perfect solution for hiding away any unsightly garden clutter. **BOTTOM** The clear-cut garden structure is softened by the use of romantic planting, such as pastel-coloured tulips, wild strawberries and Mexican fleabane (*Erigeron karvinskianus*).

"It's always my desire to create little nooks to hang out in and places to perch in a garden, no matter how small it is. Although the raised beds were principally designed with the aesthetic role of bringing dynamism to the garden, they also carve out different areas that allow the garden to be occupied and used in different ways – to eat, to lounge, to play and to hide."

MIRIA HARRIS

The Power of Simplicity
BUTTER WAKEFIELD

———

The best-designed spaces are often based on principles of simple, but not simplistic, design. Here, garden designer Butter Wakefield shows her complete understanding of form, texture and, above all, composition. Her confident use of topiary forms showcases how the most enchanting spaces can be created with a limited palette of plants. At the end of the garden, cloud-pruned Japanese holly (*Ilex crenata*) specimens are a counterpoint to a river birch (*Betula nigra*). This striking multistemmed tree, positioned to one side, forms a single mass with trees from the neighbouring garden. It also breaks up the grid and suggests some informality in an otherwise quite symmetrical composition. The planting is predominantly green using clearly defined shapes, with the soft foliage of lady's mantle (*Alchemilla mollis*), geraniums and hydrangeas in between.

OPPOSITE Iconic Crittall windows divide the garden into a series of breathtakingly beautiful vignettes that can be enjoyed from the dining room.

ABOVE Butter has used a highly restricted number of species to create the garden, but the result is an intriguing, sculptural and enchanting space.

An Edited Palette

• A limited palette of plants radiates confidence and style. Clipped topiary forms create a powerful rhythm through this garden and a strong winter structure. The varying sizes of the spheres produces an undulating effect, providing additional interest, while hydrangeas and geraniums dotted in between soften an otherwise formal look.

• Planting a large tree in a small space may seem counterintuitive but, if done carefully, it can make your garden feel much bigger by introducing a different scale and proportion.

• A garden doesn't have to be big to adopt this look. Cloud-pruned Japanese holly (*Ilex crenata*) trees planted in large planters will look incredible in any space, whether a small courtyard, a roof terrace or even a lightwell. Planting them next to large pots of white hydrangeas will achieve a similar look and feel.

• Clay pavers laid on their sides provide an elegant, discreet backdrop to the planting. Their dark colour contrasts with the different shades of green, providing depth and a sense of mystery.

ABOVE The showy blooms of white hydrangeas float above the rest of the plants, providing the highlights to an otherwise all-green fabric of foliage.

ABOVE Planted in a large terracotta pot, the cloud-pruned Japanese holly is a living sculpture – ever-changing and evolving, providing year-round interest.

ABOVE The canopy of the large river birch is light and semi-transparent. It provides dappled shade in a confined space without overwhelming it with heavy shadow.

"One of my favourite clients and gardens – I adore how leafy and geometric it is. One would never guess it is located in the middle of the city."

BUTTER WAKEFIELD

RIGHT Topiary box balls are pruned to perfection and interplanted with soft feathery plants. Their contrasting textures and forms provide beautifully balanced compositions. BELOW A generous, circular wooden table, positioned in the dappled shade of the river birch, provides a perfect setup for outdoor dining.

Outdoor Room
CAMERON LANDSCAPES & GARDENS

—

A garden can become an integral part of a house and, at times, the most important room. The form of this house suggests that one could not exist without the other, and the two work together in perfect harmony. The garden, designed by Cameron Landscapes & Gardens, sits three steps proud of the kitchen floor and mimics the interior space effortlessly. Herringbone-brick paving resembles an outdoor version of an almost identical coloured wooden floor inside the house, obscuring the inside-outside boundary even further. The planting is a complex play of texture and form in different shades of green, proof that a painterly planting scheme need not involve an abundance of colour; the use of textural foliage and plants of varying shapes and sizes can be just as effective. It is simply beautiful and brings informality to an otherwise angular space.

OPPOSITE ABOVE The garden, situated just a few steps above the floor level of the property, makes the house appear as if it has been carved out of the surrounding landscape.
OPPOSITE BELOW The herringbone pattern used for the interior floor has been continued throughout the lower and upper terraces with brick paving.
RIGHT White hydrangeas are one of very few flowering plants found in this garden, which otherwise mostly relies on the clever use of textural foliage.

Shades of Green

—

• Make room for plants in the smallest of corners. Large stone block steps are inlaid with creeping ground-cover plants and every empty patch of hard surface is covered in an abundance of pots that soften the edges and create moments of beauty.

• Comfortable, high-quality furniture is a worthwhile investment, highlighting the style of a garden and making it much more inviting. Here, two large chairs and a bistro-style table just outside the kitchen provide the perfect spot for morning coffee, while a lounge-style sofa on the upper terrace is an invitation for a cosy and relaxing evening.

• There's a strong design language dialogue between the interior and exterior spaces. The herringbone brick paving showcases how colour and pattern can be used to create a sense of continuity.

• The colour palette of the planting is hues of green with a limited number of white flowers. The beauty of the planting is expressed through the use of texture and form. A selection of leathery leaf ferns, coarse topiary and exotic climbers provide an intricate fabric of foliage.

ABOVE The absence of colour in the garden is compensated for by the richness of textures used in the planting as well as the hardscaping.

ABOVE Solid stone blocks, interplanted with creeping ground-cover plants and ferns for a softening effect, have been used to create striking steps to the upper terrace.

ABOVE White bacopa flowers scattered among finely textured leaves are perfect for trailing over walls or covering empty patches under larger specimens.

"We loved designing this north-facing garden, creating an outdoor room that is a seamless extension of the kitchen. The planting itself is visually stimulating with different textures, leaf shapes and levels, which all provide focal points. The garden really comes alive at night with the use of creative lighting."

ALASDAIR CAMERON

ABOVE Contemporary lounge chairs and a small coffee table create the perfect breakfast spot, extending the kitchen out into the garden. **LEFT** The narrow linear space between the glazing of the kitchen and the garden wall has been used to display a variety of pots with characterful plant specimens.

Container Cottage Garden
CHARLIE McCORMICK

It is almost impossible to imagine that someone could turn a tiny urban roof terrace, measuring just under 20 sq m (215 sq ft), into a charming and luscious cottage-style garden. Yet, this small container garden, designed by Charlie McCormick, is much more than just a piece of the countryside brought into the city. It is a functional and productive outdoor area, which showcases how small-scale container gardening can elevate a living space to new heights. Containers provide flexibility for those who one day might want to relocate their garden to a different home. Instead of being limiting, container gardening allows room for error and experimentation with different styles of planting. As proven by this striking garden, extravagant flowers, culinary herbs and even a productive apple tree can all thrive where least expected.

OPPOSITE This small terrace is covered in tall and voluminous plants, creating a powerful visual impact and the sense of a much larger space.

ABOVE There is a preconception that apple and fig trees, even grapevines, should only be grown in a country garden. This urban rooftop proves otherwise.

Character Building

• Plant a mixture of cosmos, lavender, foxgloves and lupins for a joyful and informal look. Experiment with growing herbs, vegetables and fruit in large containers for the full cottage-garden experience.

• The best approach to creating a container garden full of character is to think outside the box. Visit vintage fairs and antique shops where you are most likely to find an eclectic mix of furniture and design pieces. Look out for vintage crates and large, weathered wooden, metal or terracotta pots and ornaments that could double up as planters.

• Containers can dry out fairly quickly, especially in hot summers. Consider installing a simple automated watering system if your schedule doesn't allow for regular tending. Bear in mind that some materials are a lot more weatherproof than others, and that the smaller the container, the more likely it is to dry out.

• Trellis panels create privacy without blocking the light out completely. Plant clematis or jasmine to cover the panels in lush green foliage and fill the air with a delicious fragrance.

ABOVE Colourful dahlias are planted in containers that hang over the side of the terrace railings.

ABOVE Climbing plants cover trellis panels around the terrace, providing privacy with evergreen foliage and seasonal flowers.

ABOVE Terracotta pots of various shapes and sizes are dotted throughout the space and create layers of interest and intrigue.

LEFT AND ABOVE An impressive collection of small pots, arranged on an antique marble-top table, showcases an array of sedums and cacti.
TOP The blowsy blooms of agapanthus and foxgloves, typically seen in cottage gardens, look just as comfortable and at home on this roof terrace.

LEFT Agapanthus makes for an impressive pot plant in small gardens and is surprisingly sturdy when it comes to exposed rooftop conditions. **BELOW** The upper terrace has been turned into an exquisite productive garden. The limited space allows more time for tending the plants. **OPPOSITE** Vintage-style furniture in a vibrant yellow provides a splash of colour and a sense of rustic charm.

"Our tiny roof garden is almost too small to be 'designed' – it sort of is what it is! But my inspiration is always to have it as full and as ebullient as possible. Plants up there need to be hardy to survive, but they also need plenty of love and attention. It's extraordinary what we have been able to grow."

— CHARLIE McCORMICK

Clear-cut Minimalism
ADOLFO HARRISON

—

Minimalist at first glance, this beautiful small courtyard is full of carefully considered details. It appears spacious and free of clutter, with the built-in furniture forming an intrinsic part of the design. Its designer, Adolfo Harrison, has turned frequently overlooked design considerations into key design features. A custom-built Western Red Cedar fence is one of the more noticeable, its large panels creating a continuous herringbone pattern that radiates warmth and craftsmanship. The benches around the courtyard perimeter are made of the same wood. Corten steel has been used for the raised beds as well as the sculptural planters filled with luscious green foliage. The larger shrub planting includes *Hydrangea aspera* subsp. *sargentiana*, *Hydrangea quercifolia* 'Snow Queen' and *Mahonia eurybracteata* 'Soft Caress', with *Vinca minor* providing ground-cover interest.

OPPOSITE This small space is an exquisite example of integrated design – every line and design element is deliberate and carefully considered.

ABOVE "The key to this project was introducing a bay window in the side return to merge both the indoors and out, ensuring the garden could be enjoyed all year round, night and day." Adolfo Harrison

Integrated Look

• Tumbled limestone paving in perfect alignment and a variety of shades creates an eye-catching exterior carpet. It looks brilliant with the ever-changing pools of light flooding through the tree canopy above.

• Built-in furniture is a great way to achieve a unified, clutter-free garden, especially where space is limited. Make the most out of it by supersizing seating areas and creating high-quality and comfortable pieces of furniture you wouldn't be able to buy off the shelf.

• If you're planning to keep the vertical surfaces of an outdoor space exposed, it's important to make them aesthetically pleasing because they are likely to be visible from indoors.

• A single large planting bed usually has greater impact than a number of small ones. Position the bed where it can be enjoyed from inside the house as well as outside. Evergreen shrubs such as late-flowering *Mahonia eurybracteata* 'Soft Caress' with its intricate foliage will provide interest in autumn and winter, and won't require much tending. Plant it alongside other plants with seasonal interest for a year-round display.

ABOVE The limited palette of materials, plants and objects in this garden is outweighed by the exquisite craftsmanship and meticulous, custom-designed details.

ABOVE Star jasmine (*Trachelospermum jasminoides*) climbers are rooted in large, corten-steel planters, which develop a unique patina over time.

ABOVE Instead of dotting a number of small plants throughout the space, Adolfo has created a generously sized single planting bed, which has a greater impact.

RIGHT Large wooden seating platforms, designed specifically for the space, convey a sense of luxuriousness.
BELOW Tumbled limestone paving in a variety of shades introduces a subtle informality and playfulness to an otherwise minimalist design.

Glamorous and Edgy
ABIGAIL AHERN

—

Smooth and curvy chairs, crunched-up leather seats, a shiny table
and a grand chandelier sound like the description of a glamorous
yet edgy living room. And in a way it is, only this one is under the
open sky, outside interior design guru Abigail Ahern's extraordinary
home. In this outdoor room, she seems to be breaking many garden
design myths with her ingenious use of colour, objects and scale.
Dark colours provide a sense of luxury against lush green foliage.
The black garden studio tucked away at the end of the garden looks
like a secret hideaway, cosy and mysterious. It is enveloped in tall
trees that make the garden feel grander. Perhaps one of the most
unexpected elements is the chandelier. It would appear that the
secret to creating an exciting outdoor room which is both luxurious
and eclectic lies in contrasting layers of texture, scale and objects.

OPPOSITE There are so many design ideas that seem
to have spilled from the living room into the courtyard
that the only boundary separating the two is the
double-height wall of Crittall windows.

ABOVE The design of the garden is derived from
Abigail's interior design expertise and goes beyond
any preconception of what a garden should be and
how it should look.

An Interior Approach

• Like the adjacent indoor room, the colours of the garden are mostly muted and dark, including black and a variety of greys. They enhance the sense of sophistication and luxury. The dark inky tones also provide an excellent backdrop for the plants, highlighting the vibrant greens of the foliage.

• The unexpected use of different textures for the furniture in this garden is ingenious, exciting and playful. The same textural treatment is used for the planting. The varied patterns and surfaces of the smooth, glossy, rough or irregular foliage result in an array of greens that provides lots of interest without being too obvious.

• Don't rule out anything that is typically never seen in a garden – it might just become the key feature, like the extravagant chandelier or indoor sofa used here.

• The slightly overgrown and unkempt look of the garden is achieved by allowing plants to grow and develop naturally, resulting in a space that is unique, characterful and charming.

ABOVE Tall black bamboo with its luscious foliage has been used to provide screening from the neighbouring properties.

ABOVE An extravagant chandelier hanging from a branch above the coffee table is a true attention grabber.

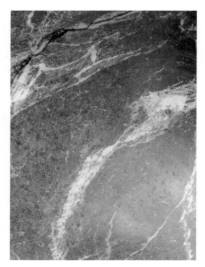

ABOVE A number of high-quality objects and materials, such as marble, add a touch of luxury to this outdoor space.

RIGHT The dark colour tones and contrasting textures in Abigail's home are also seen in the garden.

FAR RIGHT There is a relaxed feel to the garden. Nothing is perfectly aligned or pruned, and plants are left to grow naturally and truly inhabit the space.

BELOW Abigail believes that you can never overdose on texture, and this design principle is reflected in the garden through the unexpected choices of materials and finishes.

BELOW RIGHT Quirky pieces of furniture are dotted throughout the space, creating an "Alice in Wonderland" feel – intriguing, mysterious and full of soul.

OVERLEAF The colour palette of the planting is predominantly shades of green, with the shape and textural qualities of the plants providing year-round interest. **PAGE 110** A narrow garden path lined with grasses and surrounded by trees on both sides leads to a secluded garden studio at the far end of the garden. **PAGE 111** Finding unique and characterful garden furniture may be a tricky task at times. It's always worth checking interior furniture stores for pieces that would also be suitable outdoors.

"My garden is incredibly restorative; it's a place where I can go sit and chill at the end the day in the summer, rejuvenate, cook and feel in harmony with nature. I've designed it so I never see the neighbours, and there are lots of little areas to sit in. Texture is key and a restrained colour palette is fundamental, as is scent. So jasmine, lilac and herbs scent the air in the warmer months, with bay and mimosa scenting the air in the cooler months. I use the garden all year round, summer and winter. It's my refuge and my happy place."

ABIGAIL AHERN

"It's not often that someone asks you to turn a 1.2-m (4-ft) wide space into a garden, especially when it is six floors up above the ground. To see it undergo such a transformation and breathe life into it was a very challenging task, but also incredibly rewarding."
ULA MARIA

Style

City Oasis
ULA MARIA

—

Balconies are often awkward shapes, either narrow and long or wide and short, yet wonderful gardens can still be created on them. Plants often grow where we least expect them, and it may be surprising how much you can do with a tiny space. With this 1.2-m (4-ft) wide balcony, I hoped to show that unconventional spaces don't have to be boring or remain unused, nor do they have to keep to traditional plant choices. With a touch of imagination and big ambition, they can be turned into a tropical oasis, with spaces to grow, cook, dine or simply relax. Here, festoon lights that zigzag the length of the balcony exaggerate the horizontal lines, suggesting greater width. Layers of plants at different heights and a variety of pot sizes create depth, softening an otherwise harsh balustrade boundary. This is an urban jungle taken to new heights!

OPPOSITE The materials and colour palette used for the balcony complement the building's architecture. Tropical, hardy plants enrich the space, as do the abundant grasses on the neighbours' terrace above.

ABOVE Robust and easy to care for, the dwarf Chusan palm (*Trachycarpus wagnerianus*) introduces height to the narrow balcony, framing the attractive views of the city but without obstructing them.

Tropical Jungle

- A shady terrace exposed to harsh winds can be tricky to turn into a green oasis, but not impossible. Plants such as *Fatsia japonica*, *Pittosporum tenuifolium* and dwarf Chusan palm (*Trachycarpus wagnerianus*) will withstand some of the toughest growing conditions while providing you with an urban jungle in exchange for minimal care.

- It might seem counterintuitive to introduce large specimens to a very constrained space but, in most cases, they will make it appear bigger, with their foliage beginning above eye level. In this terrace garden, the wide spread of the dwarf Chusan palm canopy overhangs the space, creating the illusion of greater width.

- Bamboo can enclose a space in an abundance of tropical foliage and provide dense screening from neighbours. There are many types of bamboo to choose from that vary in colour and size. They are great plants for providing height without requiring much room to grow.

- The rattan swing chair, like a cocoon nestled among the tall tropical plants, is a brilliant way to enjoy the city skyline at night.

ABOVE Colourful furniture and accessories brighten the otherwise muted colour palette of the shady terrace as well as introducing an element of fun.

ABOVE The cocooning swing chair, positioned against tall bamboo plants to provide shelter, makes a cosy spot for reading and relaxing.

ABOVE Industrial-style wall lights provide atmospheric lighting at night, while festoon lights zigzagging across the balcony create the illusion of a wider space.

ABOVE A contemporary interpretation of a traditional Victorian dolly tub-style planter, made out of durable fibre clay, mimics the pattern and colour of the balcony floor.

ABOVE RIGHT The plants chosen are able to withstand the harsh temperatures and strong winds that can be experienced on a rooftop.

RIGHT The planting palette includes *Fatsia japonica*, *Pittosporum tenuifolium*, bamboo, *Trachycarpus wagnerianu*s and a variety of ferns.

Playing with Shapes and Patterns
GEORGIA LINDSAY

———

It's not an easy task to turn a small outdoor space into somewhere attractive and welcoming when bikes, bins (garbage cans) and cars are part of the mix. But this compact urban courtyard by Georgia Lindsay has all the practical paraphernalia hidden away. The storage is so well integrated into the space that it's almost invisible. Intricately patterned fretwork panels, which cast dramatic shadows throughout the day, enclose the seating area and offer privacy while still allowing in the light. The subtle colour spectrum gives an overall unified look, with the bright green planting dotted around providing bursts of life and seasonal interest. Suspended between two planters is a wooden bench, reinforcing the garden's integrated look. It appears to float above the skilfully laid "tile rug" that denotes the centre of this outdoor room.

OPPOSITE The small seating area, surrounded by plants, has become an extension of the interior living space, with a built-in floating bench and coffee table.

ABOVE The seating area is enclosed with a Moorish-style screen, which provides a degree of privacy while still allowing natural light to enter the restricted space.

Small and Multifunctional

—

• The bike shed, which houses four bikes, has been given a green roof, which is an excellent way to integrate an otherwise unsightly structure into the garden.

• The colours of the garden are mostly shades of grey, from warm clay to cool metallic tones. The unified colour palette creates a space that feels calm and relaxing.

• Privacy can be difficult to achieve in a small urban garden. Courtyards are often overlooked by neighbouring properties, which makes them less inviting. Fretwork panels provide attractive screening in the seating area, emphasizing the intimacy of the space, while still allowing light to filter through. They also double up as an exquisite support for climbing plants.

• A small "rug" has been created using exterior tiles to denote the core of the courtyard. It resembles an indoor living room carpet and creates a focal point that draws attention to the carefully thought-out space, away from the urban surroundings.

Style

ABOVE Looking out over the green roof of the bike shed, the clients, who live on the two upper floors, can appreciate the garden from a distance as well as close up.

ABOVE Intriguing monochrome tiles, resembling a rug with a bold geometric pattern, anchor the seating zone and focus the eye.

ABOVE Contemporary grey stools complement the overall monochromatic colour palette. Their asymmetrical top-to-bottom form looks informal yet slick.

"This awkward L-shaped backyard presented several challenges. Accessed down wrought-iron stairs, it had to accommodate a car parking space, bike shed and bin store, as well as an attractive seating area. The storage area beyond the stairs also needed screening – a lot to fit into the 40 sq m (430 sq ft) space. The hard landscaping has a bold monochromatic palette off-setting the planting against the panels' deep shades."

GEORGIA LINDSAY

LEFT Three custom-made fibreglass planters make generous-sized containers for the lime-green and plum planting palette. **TOP** The stairs have been clad with artificial maidenhair ferns to conceal the storage area behind them. **ABOVE** The custom-made fretwork panels emphasize the intimacy of the seating area, while at the same time screening the car and bins (garbage cans) from view.

An Enchanting Studio Garden
THE LAND GARDENERS

—

Calm and tranquil are perhaps two of the most overworked words used for describing gardens. However, the dreamy studio garden of The Land Gardeners – Henrietta Courtauld and Bridget Elworthy – is truly worthy of them. The material and colour palette is subtle and refined. Nothing is overpowering and everything works together in perfect harmony. Giant melianthus, climbing courgettes (zucchini), fennel, figs and mint burst out of this small but very productive urban jungle in the middle of the city. The garden becomes a centrepiece to be enjoyed from both the house and the studio, which is located in the shed at the end of the garden. Plants are mostly tall, obscuring the views towards each end of the garden and tricking the eye into thinking the space is larger. These tall plants also work in harmony with the surrounding large trees in the neighbouring gardens.

OPPOSITE Soft clouds of *Hydrangea arborescens* 'Annabelle' float above the rest of the planting, obscuring the view of the garden between the house and studio, making the space appear larger.

ABOVE Theatrical floor to ceiling-height curtains open up to unveil a picture-perfect courtyard in all its beauty.

Productive and Pretty

———

• Flowers for cutting can be planted throughout the garden or within a specifically dedicated area. Dahlias, peonies and sweet peas make incredible seasonal cut flowers, while eryngiums, hydrangeas or achilleas are perfect dried and displayed in winter.

• When planning your garden, you should always think about the journey you wish to create through it. Tall plants or features will help either to obscure views or frame vistas, without revealing the whole garden at the first encounter.

• The material palette of the garden is distilled and minimalistic. High-quality materials used for the hardscape give a timeless structure to the garden. This allows the plants to take centre stage and become the focus through the seasons.

• A garden shed can be much more than simply a storage space for outdoor tools. It has the potential to be turned into the most beautiful studio space. With a desk facing the garden, here the studio is a sanctuary for both work and daydreaming.

ABOVE Antiques markets are excellent places for sourcing unique pieces, such as this vintage green metal bench, at reasonable prices.

ABOVE Deep grey York stone cobbles provide an attractive and distinctive backdrop to this studio garden, enhancing the overall relaxed atmosphere.

ABOVE Buckets of cut dahlias and branches of rosemary, ready for flower arrangements, enliven the space with their bright blooms and delicious scent.

"The studio is our work studio for The Land Gardeners, where we do all the design work for our gardens. We focus on designing productive gardens. Hence we have tried to weave as many productive plants into this garden as we can – figs, fennel, mint, climbing beans, courgettes [zucchini], basil, salads – as well as cutting flowers. Even in this small space we are able to gather hydrangeas and roses."

THE LAND GARDENERS

ABOVE The sculptural shape of fennel (*Foeniculum vulgare*) makes it the perfect choice for flower arrangements. The slender stems and delicate yellow crowns radiate elegance and romance. **BELOW** Woven fence panels, made out of coppiced willow, promote ideas of craftsmanship and sustainability. **RIGHT** A narrow garden path leading to The Land Gardeners' studio at the far end of the garden is enveloped by plants, creating the sense of an immersive journey through the space.

An Enchanting Studio Garden

LEFT *Melianthus major*, with its strong architectural form, makes a dramatic specimen plant in a sunny spot. Here, it is speckled with the deep burgundy flowers of a sanguisorba.

BELOW Eccentric yellow antique chairs, paired with the green-tiled coffee table, enliven the balcony with a playful burst of colour.

OPPOSITE Even though the garden is small, it is big enough to produce a plentiful crop of flowers for cutting, with *Hydrangea arborescens* 'Annabelle' taking centre stage.

An Enchanting Studio Garden

Plant Hunter's Dream

JACK WALLINGTON

—

Stepping into Jack Wallington's garden feels as if you are opening a plant hunter's case. Full of exotic plants, it is bound to awaken every visitor's curiosity. Designed by Jack, this urban jungle is filled with jewels of purple and pink blooms amid clusters of unusual foliage. Every corner is a joyous display of the unexpected, with each plant carefully placed to suit its needs. When the collection ranges from showy dahlias to tropical bananas and dry-climate cacti, it's no surprise that most plants here are in pots, just in case they get cold feet in winter and need to be moved inside. There are so many great things about growing plants in pots, but perhaps the most exciting is being able to rearrange your garden as often as you like. And if things don't turn out as expected, it is much easier to replace potted plants and transform your garden for the following season.

OPPOSITE The long, narrow path to the side of the property is bordered by a collection of rare, unusual and mostly tropical plants.
ABOVE LEFT Jack hasn't replaced the hardscaping since moving in, but has instead focused on establishing a spectacular plant display.

ABOVE RIGHT Large bifold doors reveal an awe-inspiring view of the garden, reminiscent of a giant Victorian botanical painting.

Tropical Pinks and Purples

• Most of the flowers in this garden are in shades of purple and pink. Identifying a colour scheme from the outset helps to create a garden that appears unified and considered.

• Water features come in all shapes and sizes. No matter how small, they have the potential to home an abundance of wildlife and plants. Almost any planter can be turned into a water feature without breaking the bank. You will be surprised at the range of water plants out there!

• The plants in this garden are mostly tropical, with theatrical foliage providing year-round interest. Creating your very own collection of plants is a great way of dipping your feet into the gardening world.

• As well as being spaces for relaxation, gardens should be engaging and fun too. Think of yours as a creative space in which to experiment and discover the joy of growing things and reconnecting with nature. Ask yourself what types of plants and landscapes arouse your curiosity, and don't be afraid to get things wrong the first time round – even the best gardeners will tell you that the "perfect" garden doesn't exist.

ABOVE The colour palette of the flower planting, which is mostly shades of pink and purple, is accompanied by a range of foliage plants of different hues and shapes.

ABOVE Dahlias are wonderful flowers for providing late-summer to early-autumn interest, when most other plants have finished flowering.

ABOVE The large tropical leaves of the banana plant make a striking summer display, but these are best grown in pots where temperatures fall below 7°C (45°F).

LEFT The tiny pond in a zinc container is full of life, with *Eriophorum angustifolium*, *Iris* 'Black Gamecock' and *Nymphaea* 'Laydekeri Fulgens' – a hardy water lily – all thriving.

BELOW LEFT Jack hasn't missed an opportunity to grow plants everywhere he possibly can, including in a charming terracotta planter perched on a windowsill.

> "We have a one-bed ground-floor apartment, which we converted to open out onto the small patio garden. It isn't a designed garden at all – the paving was there long before we bought the apartment – but I have filled it with as many of my favourite plants as possible, to create a colourful jungle in which I can propagate and observe how things grow."
>
> JACK WALLINGTON

RIGHT Although there is little furniture in the garden, the two contemporary metal rocking chairs provide enough flexibility and comfort to allow for quiet relaxation and enjoyment of the space.

RIGHT The garden boundaries are completely covered in plants, with their showy flowers poking above the fence, to be enjoyed by neighbours. **BELOW** The unique collection of plants continues indoors, where it is just as impressive, with a continuation of the pink and purple colour scheme. **OPPOSITE** Dozens of terracotta pots filled with exotic plants are dotted around the garden.

Vintage French
GABRIELLE SHAY

—

There is something quite magical about the higgledy-piggledy
streets of French villages, with their clusters of vintage bistro
furniture, reclaimed materials and home frontages overgrown
with deliciously scented climbers. The key to creating a charming
French vintage look is layering, and this London garden by Gabrielle
Shay has it down to a tee. Layers of planting have been gradually
added, resulting in a textured tapestry of plants. Similarly, the trees
surrounding the plot have been used as a green backdrop for some
antique furniture, creating depth and intrigue. On the balcony, the
planters in front of the railing soften the boundary and draw the
greenery indoors. In summer, the front of the house is studded with
thousands of white star jasmine (*Trachelospermum jasminoides*)
flowers, which fill the air with their sweet perfume.

OPPOSITE ABOVE Trailing nasturtiums, pelargoniums
and hydrangeas soften the hard lines of the balcony.
OPPOSITE BELOW Vintage furniture in clusters around
the garden provides a variety of seating options.

ABOVE The steps to the front door are immersed in
green, with ground-cover plants cushioned between
stone slabs, the walls covered in climbers and a
variety of planters spilling over with plants.

Layered Look

• Plant scented climbing plants in front of the house to greet you and your visitors with their delicious fragrance. White star jasmine (*Trachelospermum jasminoides*), *Clematis montana*, *Akebia quinata* or *Clematis armandii* are some of the most popular choices.

• Mix and match vintage furniture and pots of different colours, sizes and forms to create garden rooms. Create seating in otherwise unused parts of the garden, and surround bistro-style furniture with pots of flowers to make the space even more welcoming.

• Create layers by placing clusters of planters in front of the more established trees and shrubs. A variety of characterful vintage layers will evoke the sense of a garden that has been established over many years or even by many generations.

• Old wooden crates can make stylish planters. Placed on the balcony floor, they help to disguise the railings and create a link to the wider landscape. Place them in rows for greater impact and plant with an abundance of flowers or vegetables and edible plants.

ABOVE Encouraged to spread and reclaim the hardscape structures, ground-creeping plants thrive in every corner of the garden.

ABOVE With echoes of the countryside, woven panels made out of willow complement the vintage garden look.

ABOVE An antique urn at the entrance to the house greets visitors with a seasonal display of flowers.

"This garden is one that is constantly evolving, not just maintained. Over time we've gradually added layers of planting, creating a textured, rich plant tapestry. We focused on climbers because, as with many London gardens, space is precious and limited. Some may find these multilayered plantings messy, but they provide more for wildlife. Seating corners and clusters of pots were used to make the garden look more intentional and less intimidating for those more comfortable with traditional manicured gardens."

GABRIELLE SHAY

ABOVE LEFT Star jasmine definitely lives up to its name by outshining every other plant, with its white star-shaped flowers encasing the house. **TOP** Vintage wooden crates with their weathered appearance make wonderful planters that always bring a touch of rustic charm to a space. **ABOVE** The neutral earthy colours of these natural stone and galvanized steel dolly pots blend into their green surroundings seamlessly, as if they have always been there.

OPPOSITE In this beautiful and elegant display of white blooms and green foliage, *Hydrangea macrophylla* 'Lanarth White' shares a generous metal container with an underplanting of *Pelargonium* 'White Strigofolium' and trailing vinca.
LEFT A variety of pots and planters covers the perimeter of the balcony, obscuring the railings and creating a link to the surrounding greenery.
BELOW Placed among a cluster of pots and in the shelter of overhead greenery, a vintage wooden bench provides a tranquil place to sit.

137

Vintage French

Furnish

PAVING

One of the first design considerations when creating a garden is the paving. Whether for a patio, path or terrace, the paving helps to define how the outdoor space will be used and forms its primary structure. Pathways lead us from one space to another, both physically and visually, linking some of the most used parts of a garden. In the winter months, when deciduous plants expose the bones of the garden, paving often becomes the most dominant feature, so it's imperative for it to be not only functional but also aesthetically pleasing. It's important for all aspects of paving to be carefully considered: size, layout, material, texture and colour. They will all influence the overall style of the outdoor space and the experience to be had.

• When selecting hardscape materials for your outdoor space, always explore different finish options. There's a wide spectrum of textural qualities that can be achieved using the same material, from smooth and soft to rough and uneven. Note that texture will also affect the colour of the material too.

ABOVE LEFT Victorian mosaic tiles form a strong focal point at the centre of this garden and define the seating area. **LEFT** Many paving materials come in an assortment of different colours and sizes, and can be used as a mix to form intricate patterns and layouts. **ABOVE** It is important to consider the relationship of intersecting materials. Here, soft brown planks of wood complement the warm tones of clay bricks.

• If your outdoor space is limited, consider using the same materials indoors and out to create a unified, cohesive design that will lead the eye and make the space appear bigger than it actually is. Most indoor materials such as stone, wood or brick will be suitable for outdoor use, but will most likely require special treatment to be able to withstand the elements.

• Depending on the design, paving is often the most expensive element of a garden. Where the budget is limited, it is always good practice to invest in high-quality paving for the areas that will be used and seen the most. Alternative, more cost-effective materials that share the same colour or textural qualities could be selected for the areas or paths that won't be used or seen on a regular basis.

• Before selecting your paving materials, consider the architectural properties of your home as well as the vernacular architecture. The wider context must be taken into consideration – imposing something that is alien to the site is always going to look unnatural and forced. Locally sourced materials often work really well.

FAR LEFT Make sure you research the different ways that a material can be used; it will have an impact on the overall look and feel of a space.
LEFT Reclaimed materials, such as these York stone cobbles, are brilliant for introducing lots of character and charm into a brand new space, while remaining discreet and timeless.
BELOW The palette of hardscape materials is often inspired by the architecture or materials used for the interior. These red brick slips have been laid both in and outside the property.

WATER

Water is a symbol of life and is bound to enhance any outdoor space. There's something magical about the sound of trickling water. It brings a sense of calm and wellbeing, and is both relaxing and energizing. A water feature doesn't have to be huge or monumental to have a big impact and be enjoyed by people as well as wildlife. It is the movement and sound of water that offers a completely unique aspect to a space. There are water features for even the most difficult spaces, such as small balconies or roof gardens, that can help you escape the hustle and bustle of the city as soon as you close your eyes.

• Different sound qualities appeal to different people. The sound of moving water is undeniably appealing, but there are those who prefer a gentle trickling, while others might associate a trickle with the irritating sound of a dripping tap and prefer a more forceful sound. Likewise, the noise of faster-flowing water might be overpowering in the wrong setting.

• Water appeals to wildlife and will attract even the most discreet of city inhabitants, which are otherwise hard to spot. Water plants or boulders that sit just above the water will encourage frogs and insects, while small elevated features will attract birds.

• Wall-mounted water features are brilliant for gardens where there is limited space. They provide all of the benefits of a typical water feature without taking up much of the precious space. Consider installing a wall-mounted water feature with a reflective surface to create the illusion of a bigger space.

• Think of your outdoor space as a whole when selecting a water feature. Clearly defined, formal shapes, such as a rectangles, squares or circles, tend to work better in an urban setting, whereas naturalistic and rustic-looking water features can look completely out of place and superimposed in a modern city garden if they have not been incorporated with enough care.

FAR LEFT A burgundy-coloured bowl, turned into a water feature, bursts with life with an abundance of tropical aquatic plants. LEFT Concealing a water feature among plants creates a sense of intrigue and anticipation. BELOW Some of the most effective water features are the simplest. This large metal pond nestled among plants produces a striking, mirror-like effect.

STORAGE

Outdoor storage is often an afterthought rather than a well-considered design decision, but it shouldn't be. Storage units can be beautiful as well as functional. In fact, they are no different from any other item of furniture, and could even become beautifully crafted focal points. There are many other ways of incorporating storage into an outdoor space besides the conventional shed, filled with long-forgotten garden paraphernalia. Outdoor cabinets, storage benches, skilfully built log shelves and even upcycled furniture might be a much better way to achieving an uncluttered and spacious garden.

• The wealth of high-quality gardening tools available to choose from can be overwhelming. Some of these tools have been crafted so beautifully that it is a shame to hide them away in the depths of a garden shed. Instead, consider displaying them on a garden wall, organized on wall-mounted shelves or a shelf ladder.

• In situations where a garden shed is required, consider the scale and form that is most appropriate. Sheds come in all shapes and sizes, from wide and low to tall and narrow. The latter works well if you have a variety of tall garden tools such as spades, forks and brushes to store away.

• Using multifunctional furniture and items can help you maximize your garden's potential if you have a limited amount of space. Benches, chairs and even coffee tables could be designed to double up as storage units.

• It's quite common for a small urban garden to be turned into what could only be described as "storage space". Everything from bikes and unused furniture to bins (garbage cans) and gardening tools seem to slowly take over, leaving little space for enjoyment. Consider carefully how much storage space you will require right from the start of the design process and how best to incorporate it into your garden.

BELOW Carefully considered storage is integrated into the design of a fireplace, resulting in a beautiful display of logs.
RIGHT Garden storage need not be dull, grey and boring, as proven by this playful and contemporary take on outdoor cabinets.

RIGHT A lot of outdoor furniture can be designed to double up as storage. The wooden top of this bench opens to provide plenty of space for garden paraphernalia.

GREEN ROOFS

Green roofs have come a long way from the time when the domestic-scale systems first started to appear on the urban gardening market. Today, green roofs cover pretty much every type of garden imaginable, from low-maintenance, lightweight displays of sedums to naturalistic native wildflower meadows and biodiverse microhabitats. Aside from providing beautiful seasonal displays that can be just as eye-catching as conventional gardens, green roofs are reclaiming underused urban surfaces, allowing nature back into the city. While able to accommodate a surprising diversity of plants, they also create space for wildlife, capturing rainwater, cooling air temperatures and providing insulation to the building.

• Green roofs don't have to be large-scale to be worthwhile. An extension roof, garden shed or even the roof of a storage area can all be turned into a beautiful small-scale landscape.

• The type of green roof you decide to create should respond to site conditions, garden aspect, water needs and available soil depth. The depth of soil is particularly important, as any increase in loading will have an impact on the building structure supporting it.

• The most eco-friendly type of green roof available is referred to as a "biodiverse". Its prime function is to increase biodiversity by re-creating the local habitat replaced by the building as closely as possible. Insects are welcomed by the introduction of stone, sand and organic matter, which are left to be enveloped eventually by self-seeding plants.

• Like any other type of garden, green roofs have to be regularly maintained. Wildflower roofs are often perceived as lower maintenance but they do require removing the previous season's growth in order to encourage the spread of seed for the season to come. Most green roof specialists will be able to advise on the most suitable green roof for specific site conditions and maintenance requirements.

LEFT A green roof covers the top of the bike shed, providing a striking seasonal display of plants and wildlife. **ABOVE** Most sedums have shallow roots and are lightweight and easy to maintain, making them among the most popular plants for green roofs.

BELOW Provided they are installed correctly and regularly maintained, green roofs can be turned into the most striking and complex of planting designs.

GREEN WALLS

In recent years, we have started to understand more about the benefits that nature and gardens can bring into our lives. However, not all of us have the luxury of a large garden. The lack of nature in our concrete jungles highlights our need to be creative with every outdoor surface available, including walls. Pretty much every wall can be turned into a lush, lively, flourishing and scented garden. It can also add an aesthetic and ecological value to the property, and even be turned into a functional productive garden.

• In a similar way to green roofs, green walls can make a difference when it comes to air quality, temperature and run-off water. They can help to increase biodiversity and encourage wildlife to return to cities. They can also be designed to help with building insulation, keeping your home warmer in the winter and cooler during the hot months.

• There are some long-term obstacles to consider when thinking about installing a green wall. First, they are quite expensive to install but, more important, they are expensive to maintain. Strategies for irrigation and plant replacement must be considered from the outset of the project for a garden wall to be successful in the long term.

• Green walls can be an all-changing element in an urban garden where space is limited. Larger plants look more effective, but they also require a good amount of soil to establish themselves. The weight of the soil and the plants, particularly after watering, must be taken into account to make sure the supporting structure is strong enough.

• There are a wide range of plants that can be used in the creation of a green wall. Plants such as strawberries don't require much soil to thrive and would make the perfect plant choice in most situations. Similarly, herbs such as mint, lavender and marigold could be planted, to create a beautifully scented display, and also harvested, to be enjoyed with summer cocktails.

BELOW The simplest way of creating a green wall is the traditional one: by growing climbing or trailing plants against a wall or fence. RIGHT A luscious green wall, extending from floor to ceiling, links the interior to the outside space, blurring the boundary between the two.

RIGHT Smothering the walls of city gardens with plants not only has aesthetic value, but also the advantage of encouraging wildlife.

LIGHTING

Lighting can transform any outdoor space, helping to create just the right atmosphere and also increasing the length of time you can spend in it. It can make a garden more inviting, not only during summer but also the cold winter months. As well as being functional, lighting should enhance a visitor's experience, create intrigue and suggest movement through the space. There are so many different ways of introducing lighting to a garden and an endless list of light fittings to choose from. It's important not to flood the whole space with light. Subtlety is key to a successful lighting design. Lighting should be used to highlight key spaces, focal points and objects, whether a patio, seating area, structural planting or a water feature rather than overwhelm them.

• Consider lighting design from the outset of the design process. This way, it can be seamlessly integrated into key areas and elements such as paving, furniture, water or sculptural features, becoming an integral part of the garden rather than an underwhelming add-on.

• There are many effects achievable with different types of lighting. Use spotlights to highlight a particular design element or a specimen plant.

Furnish

BELOW Candles dotted inside the stone carvings radiate a warm light, while discreet spotlights highlight the wall features. **RIGHT** A quirky lamp hanging from a tree branch creates a focal point, with dozens of lights glowing in the background. **BELOW RIGHT** Festoon lights are brilliant for creating a relaxed, warm atmosphere, bringing to mind summer nights at festivals.

• Uplighting works well recessed into the paving, where it emphasizes paths and seating areas. To create dark silhouettes, use backlighting by placing spotlights behind a particular feature.

• If your budget is limited, concentrate on lighting the very best elements of your garden, such as water features. These look spectacular illuminated at night. Light fittings can be set among the plants near the water or set under the water level, accentuating movement and reflections.

• To achieve the most impact with lighting, try to use a variety of lighting techniques at different levels and spots within an outdoor space. Create a hierarchy of spaces by emphasizing key areas and highlighting the most significant plants of the garden, while introducing subtler, softer lights to create an overall ambience.

• Don't forget to consider colour when designing a lighting scheme – it is bound to have a huge effect on the overall mood of the garden. The cooler shades of light will make the space feel cooler, while soft yellow tones will create a warmer, cosy atmosphere. Other colour lights such as red, green or blue are tricky to make work and require very careful consideration.

RIGHT An industrial-style light, such as a large desk lamp, is mounted on the wall and extended to illuminate an outdoor dining table.

ABOVE Discreet wall-mounted light fittings are selected to match the pattern and colour of the wall, so as not to distract from the effect of the lighting itself. **RIGHT** As well as fulfilling their primary function, light fittings can also be used as decorative design elements, to help create the desired atmosphere.

FURNITURE

While we admire and appreciate beautiful gardens for their aesthetic value, it is important to remember that the primary function of a garden is to provide an outdoor space for enjoyment, relaxation and creating memories. For many of us, our most common memories relate to sitting around a fire with a group of friends, having a celebratory meal with our family or swinging in a hammock under the tree while reading a book. Every single one of those memories has a direct connection to the outdoor furniture that enhances such experiences. Furniture is an integral part of any outdoor space and shouldn't be treated as an afterthought. It can transform a space and it's important to consider it as carefully as any other element of the garden design.

• Many of us enjoy adding unique and personal touches to our home. Likewise, the smallest and simplest of details, such as an outdoor rug, soft furnishings or a tablecloth, can give a garden a unique and distinctive look, that reflects the owner's personality.

ABOVE Attractive cushions add an extra layer of comfort to these striking chairs. **ABOVE RIGHT** A colourful tablecloth transforms a simple table and chairs from ordinary to extraordinary in minutes, without the need to replace any furniture. **RIGHT** Furniture can be used to inject colour and character into any space. These weathered metal vintage chairs introduce an element of intrigue to the tranquil courtyard.

• I have always believed that if the key structural features and background materials of the garden are relaxed and unified, then the smaller details and design elements can be of a more eclectic nature, to help inject charm and character into the space.

• Comfort is just as, if not more, important as the style of furniture. Every piece should be functional as well as beautifully crafted. If furniture is not comfortable, it will take away from an outdoor experience, so make sure that you test it before you buy, as you would with any indoor furniture.

• Furniture shouldn't be just practical; it can introduce sculptural qualities to a space as well. Many garden furniture suppliers offer a wide selection of products. However, their output is nothing compared to that of interior furniture makers, and you may find an outstanding set of furniture designed for the home that is perfectly suitable for outdoors.

RIGHT High-quality, well-crafted furniture is a worthwhile investment if you wish to entertain guests outdoors on a regular basis. **BELOW** Some of the most unusual and characterful pieces of outdoor furniture are to be found online and in antiques markets.

BELOW In gardens where space is limited, especially rooftop terraces and balconies, a charming drinks trolley (cart) is an inspired solution for keeping small items neat and tidy.

CONTAINERS

Without containers, balcony and roof gardens would not be possible. Containers can provide so many opportunities for small urban gardens and courtyards, as well as for tropical plant enthusiasts. They allow us to grow pretty much anything we want and to take them from one home to the next. Containers provide opportunities for the introduction of seasonal plants such as bulbs and annuals that can be easily replaced each year if necessary, and don't require committing to a single colour or plant scheme. The variety of container types is endless and there is at least one to suit every outdoor space imaginable.

• For any planting container to succeed, there needs to be enough potting compost, a sufficient amount of moisture and good drainage. Drainage is just as important as watering levels because it allows any excess water to escape without waterlogging the soil and rotting plant roots.

ABOVE LEFT Even small containers can make a huge difference to the look and feel of a garden.
LEFT Large containers can accommodate large specimen plants, even trees, immediately transforming a space, as on this roof garden.
ABOVE Dozens of terracotta pots in an assortment of sizes display an intriguing collection of easy-to-care-for succulents.

• Galvanized steel is arguably the most subtle and unpretentious of all metals. The neutral grey colour of the metal is guaranteed to blend in well with any surroundings, allowing the planting to take centre stage. If you are ever unsure of what metal containers would suit your outdoor space best, galvanized steel is always a great choice, no matter what your style.

• Always take weight into consideration when choosing containers. Heavy containers are naturally more stable but lightweight ones are essential for roof gardens and balconies. Once filled with soil, large containers will become extremely heavy, especially after being watered or following a downpour of rain, and may simply weigh too much.

• Generally, a container should not overpower the plants in them or distract from them, unless they are used as a sculptural feature or a focal point within the space. In most cases, a container should be used as a vehicle for the plants growing in it, and these should take centre stage.

LEFT Herbs are particularly suited to container growing and are especially useful in very small outdoor spaces, such as balconies. **BELOW LEFT** Unusual planters can be used as sculptural features and focal points to add interest, colour or height to a space. **BELOW** Galvanized-steel containers are some of the most popular types of planter. Their discreet appearance works well with most garden styles, from a traditional cottage-inspired garden to a contemporary design.

Plant

PLANTS FOR
STRUCTURE

—

◀LATIN NAME: *Corylus avellana* 'Contorta'

COMMON NAME: Corkscrew hazel

IDEAL POSITION: Full sun or partial shade.

CARE: Remove dead wood in early spring.

TIPS: Corkscrew hazel's gnarled silhouette looks incredible during a cold winter. Plant it in a large container along with hellebores for a stunning seasonal display.

◀LATIN NAME: *Viburnum davidii*

COMMON NAME: David viburnum

IDEAL POSITION: Full sun to full shade.

CARE: Lightly prune in late winter or early spring to retain the dome-like shape.

TIPS: Use this robust structural plant where little else will grow. It will tolerate shade better than most plants and provide year-round interest.

◀LATIN NAME: *Laurus nobilis*

COMMON NAME: Bay tree

IDEAL POSITION: Full sun or partial shade, sheltered from strong winds.

CARE: Lightly prune in summer and feed with a slow-release fertilizer.

TIPS: Bay leaves are used in kitchens around the world, and every keen cook should have a bay tree in their garden, to provide an endless supply of aromatic leaves.

◀ LATIN NAME: *Taxus baccata*

COMMON NAME: English yew

IDEAL POSITION: Full sun or partial shade; will tolerate dry shade.

CARE: Prune in late summer or early autumn to create the desired topiary form.

TIPS: Plant as a sculptural element among naturalistic grasses and perennials or as a backdrop hedge.

◀ LATIN NAME: *Pinus mugo*

COMMON NAME: Dwarf mountain pine

IDEAL POSITION: Full sun.

CARE: Plant in a sunny spot with well-drained soil.

TIPS: Makes a great structural plant for a dry rock garden and won't require much attention, given its slow rate of growth.

LATIN NAME: *Pittosporum tenuifolium* 'Golf Ball'

COMMON NAME: Kohuhu

IDEAL POSITION: Full sun or partial shade.

CARE: This cultivar grows into a neat, rounded shape, hence its name, so doesn't require much pruning.

TIPS: An excellent compact plant, it will provide structure all year round with its fresh evergreen foliage.

LATIN NAME: *Skimmia japonica* 'Rubella'

COMMON NAME: Japanese skimmia

IDEAL POSITION: Partial to full shade.

CARE: Skimmias are easy-care plants that can be trimmed after flowering if necessary. They respond well to annual mulching with well-rotted compost

TIPS: This excellent, trouble-free plant will provide structure and colour in an autumn or winter container display.

LATIN NAME: *Carpinus betulus*

COMMON NAME: Hornbeam

IDEAL POSITION: Full sun or partial shade.

CARE: Clip in late summer or early autumn to train and maintain a neat formal hedge shape.

TIPS: The foliage of this plant turns a beautiful burnt orange colour in autumn. Plant in a position where its year-round structural interest can be appreciated.

LATIN NAME: *Ilex crenata*

COMMON NAME: Japanese holly

IDEAL POSITION: Full sun or partial shade.

CARE: Prune this shrub in late autumn to maintain its robust, structural topiary form.

TIPS: Use this pest- and disease-free holly as an alternative to box-blight prone box (*Buxus*), while achieving the same structural and aesthetic results.

LATIN NAME: *Pinus sylvestris* 'Watereri'

COMMON NAME: Dwarf Scots pine

IDEAL POSITION: Full sun or partial shade.

CARE: Plant this slow-growing, easy-care dwarf pine in well-drained soil. Once established, it is resistant to drought.

TIPS: Can be trained into bonsai shapes and looks wonderful in Japanese-inspired gardens, with its steel-blue needles and orange-brown bark.

PLANTS FOR IMPACT

———

◄LATIN NAME: *Euphorbia mellifera*

COMMON NAME: **Canary spurge**

IDEAL POSITION: Full sun or partial shade.

CARE: Remove unwanted seedlings in spring. In late spring/early summer, cut back to the desired size, especially if the plant has become leggy. The sap can irritate the skin.

TIPS: Remove the flower buds to speed up growth and increase the leaf size.

◄LATIN NAME: *Stipa gigantea*

COMMON NAME: **Golden oats**

IDEAL POSITION: Full sun.

CARE: Cut back or comb through the plant in early spring, to remove any dead foliage.

TIPS: This ornamental grass is a definite showstopper and can reach a height of 2.5 m (8 ft), given the right growing conditions.

◄LATIN NAME: *Euphorbia characias* subsp. *wulfenii*

COMMON NAME: **Mediterranean spurge**

IDEAL POSITION: Full sun.

CARE: Can cause skin and eye irritation when handled. Remove seedlings as they appear. Encourage lots of new growth by cutting back flowered stems to the base.

TIPS: Leave enough space for this plant to grow. Its statuesque form and lime-green flowers provide year-round interest.

◄LATIN NAME: *Acer palmatum* 'Atropurpureum'

COMMON NAME: **Purple Japanese maple**

IDEAL POSITION: Partial shade and sheltered.

CARE: Protect from harsh wind and long hours of blistering sun.

TIPS: In a limited space, plant this slow-grower in a container. A compact plant, it creates plenty of impact, injecting a burst of seasonal colour that's hard to beat.

◄LATIN NAME: *Lavandula angustifolia* 'Hidcote'

COMMON NAME: **English lavender 'Hidcote'**

IDEAL POSITION: Full sun.

CARE: Carefully cut back in winter without damaging the woody stems.

TIPS: This deep-coloured lavender will provide a compact structural edge to a plant bed, path or patio. Plant lavenders close to a seating area so that you can enjoy their beautiful scent to the full.

◄LATIN NAME: *Melianthus major*

COMMON NAME: **Honey flower**

IDEAL POSITION: Full sun, sheltered.

CARE: Protect in cold winters, especially where temperatures drop below freezing. Cover the soil with dry mulch. Cut back in spring to allow for the new season's growth.

TIPS: Can grow to 2 m (6½ ft) in a season, so plant in a large pot.

◀LATIN NAME: *Fatsia japonica*

COMMON NAME: Japanese aralia

IDEAL POSITION: Partial shade.

CARE: Generally a very low-maintenance plant that grows in almost any type of soil but doesn't enjoy cold winds. Exposure to long hours of direct sunlight may cause the leaves to turn yellow. Old leaves can be removed as soon as they have turned brown.

TIPS: Although considered by some to be an old-fashioned plant, the Japanese aralia can work brilliantly when used to create an exotic display alongside complementary species. It also looks impressive when planted on its own in a big container and pruned into a large statement plant.

◀LATIN NAME: *Ficus carica* 'Brown Turkey'

COMMON NAME: Fig 'Brown Turkey'

IDEAL POSITION: Full sun, sheltered.

CARE: Needs well-drained soil. For a large specimen, remove unwanted fruit to focus the plant's energy on growth.

TIPS: Planting figs in a pot and restricting the roots will increase fruit productivity, but be sure to water regularly.

LATIN NAME: *Syringa vulgaris* ▶

COMMON NAME: Lilac

IDEAL POSITION: Full sun to partial shade.

CARE: Lilacs will become leggy if left unpruned. Prune after flowering in summer in order to shape into the desired form.

TIPS: There are many different lilac cultivars that vary in flower colour and growth rate. For a small garden, choose one of the compact, slower-growing lilacs. These make an impact with their beautiful form and heavenly scented blooms, which are stunning in flower arrangements.

CLIMBERS

—

◀LATIN NAME: *Vitis coignetiae*

COMMON NAME: **Crimson glory vine**

IDEAL POSITION: Full sun to partial shade.

CARE: Plant in moist, free-draining soil. Provide support until the main structure is established and can support new growth.

TIPS: A powerful and vigorous grower, this vine can be used to quickly cover pergolas or other large garden structures.

◀LATIN NAME: *Trachelospermum jasminoides*

COMMON NAME: **Star jasmine**

IDEAL POSITION: Full sun.

CARE: After flowering, prune back to fit the available space. In frost-prone areas, grow in pots of loam-based potting compost and move to a frost-free spot in winter.

TIPS: A perfect plant for climbing garden walls or fences or for trailing over trellises and pergolas.

◀LATIN NAME: *Wisteria sinensis*

COMMON NAME: **Chinese wisteria**

IDEAL POSITION: Full sun to light shade.

CARE: Requires lots of tending, skilful pruning and training to achieve the traditional espalier form. Feed regularly with lots of well-rotted compost for an abundance of flowers.

TIPS: Buy plants in flower, as they are more likely to flower prolifically in future.

◀LATIN NAME: *Clematis armandii*

COMMON NAME: **Armand clematis**

IDEAL POSITION: Full sun to partial shade.

CARE: Plant in a sheltered spot to protect from harsh winds. Although the clematis itself enjoys being exposed to the sun, its roots prefer to be planted deeply in a cooler, moist and well-drained soil.

TIPS: Plant Armand clematis near an entrance or a seating area so that you can better enjoy its fragrant, cream-white flowers in spring and evergreen foliage all year round.

◄LATIN NAME: *Hydrangea anomala* subsp. *petiolaris*

COMMON NAME: **Climbing hydrangea**

IDEAL POSITION: Sun to shade.

CARE: Water generously until the plant is fully established in fertile soil and protect from harsh winds. Prune carefully, otherwise flowering may be reduced the next season.

TIPS: The climbing hydrangea is an excellent choice for even the shadiest part of the garden. It will provide seasonal interest with its large white intricate flowers in late spring and early summer, and cover its support with golden leaves in autumn.

LATIN NAME: *Passiflora caerulea* 'Constance Eliott'

COMMON NAME: **Passion flower**

IDEAL POSITION: Full sun to partial shade.

CARE: Plant in moist but well-drained soil, sheltered from harsh, cold winds. Cut back untidy or overcrowded stems in spring.

TIPS: There are many vibrant colour variations of this species of passion flower but it is this climber's exotic and complex flower structure that makes it stand out from the rest. White-flowering and vigorous, it will quickly cover large surfaces and work seamlessly with any colour theme.

LATIN NAME: *Schizophragma hydrangeoides* 'Moonlight'

COMMON NAME: **Japanese hydrangea vine**

IDEAL POSITION: Full sun to partial shade.

CARE: To cover a fence or wall, plant at least 50cm (20 in) away, and provide support until the main structure of the plant is established.

TIPS: The large, heart-shaped, silver leaves of this climber will provide a beautiful backdrop for any garden. Once established, it can become a star plant of the summer, when it is covered in unusual, spectacular, white flowers.

LATIN NAME: *Actinidia kolomikta*

COMMON NAME: **Kolomikta vine**

IDEAL POSITION: Full sun.

CARE: Generally easy to care for, this vine requires some support until it is established. It grows best when sheltered, in humus-rich, well-drained soil, and should be pruned in spring.

TIPS: The heart-shaped, luscious green leaves with their white and bright pink tips look as if they have been dipped in paint. Plant this vine to inject character into an otherwise pared-back, monotonous planting scheme or combine with other unusual coloured plants to create an eccentric, eclectic display.

LATIN NAME: *Clematis* 'Frances Rivis'

COMMON NAME: **Clematis 'Frances Rivis'**

IDEAL POSITION: Full sun to shade.

CARE: 'Frances Rivis' doesn't demand much looking after. As long as its roots are in a cool soil, it is guaranteed to flourish each year. It doesn't need pruning but, if necessary, a subtle trim will keep it in shape.

TIPS: Makes an ideal climbing plant for beginner gardeners and will do well in even the most exposed, cold sites. This beautiful clematis will delight you with its reliable, stunning, pastel blue flowers every year.

LATIN NAME: *Rosa* The Generous Gardener ('Ausdrawn')

COMMON NAME: **Rose The Generous Gardener**

IDEAL POSITION: Full sun to partial shade.

CARE: Plant in a pit twice as big as the rootball with some added organic matter, and allow for a generous growing space. Provide support to shape the rose into the desired form.

TIPS: Plant this rose for its beautifully fragrant, pale pink flowers. Trained onto a wall, it will fill the space with the scents of old rose, musk and myrrh.

YEAR-ROUND INTEREST

◀LATIN NAME: *Hydrangea paniculata* 'Limelight'

COMMON NAME: Hydrangea 'Limelight'

IDEAL POSITION: Full sun to partial shade.

CARE: Add plenty of garden compost to the soil before planting and allow enough space for the plant to mature. Prune in spring to enhance the new season's growth and flowering.

TIPS: The dry flower heads are popular in winter flower arrangements.

◀LATIN NAME: *Amelanchier lamarckii*

COMMON NAME: Snowy mespilus

IDEAL POSITION: Full sun to partial shade.

CARE: Remove any unhealthy or intertwined branches in winter, to achieve the desired form.

TIPS: Train into a multistemmed specimen to look incredible all year round – from white flowers in spring, berries in summer, to bright red foliage in autumn.

◀LATIN NAME: *Euphorbia amygdaloides* var. *robbiae*

COMMON NAME: Wood spurge; Mrs Robb's Bonnet

IDEAL POSITION: Partial shade.

CARE: Remove unwanted seedlings in spring to stop it becoming invasive.

TIPS: Makes excellent ground cover for difficult sites, particularly dry shade. Mix with other woodland-style plants for a naturalistic woodland display that will look brilliant in every season.

◀LATIN NAME: *Daphne odora* 'Aureomarginata'

COMMON NAME: Daphne

Ideal position: Full sun to partial shade.

CARE: This slow-growing shrub requires minimal tending and pruning, and will be happy in most types of soil, as long as it doesn't get waterlogged.

TIPS: Just a small branch of this early-flowering garden shrub will fill your home with the most delicious sweet, jasmine scent.

◀LATIN NAME: *Miscanthus sinensis* 'Gracillimus'

COMMON NAME: Eulalia

IDEAL POSITION: Full sun.

CARE: Cut back to ground level before the new season's growth appears.

TIPS: Plant this grass to extend the season of interest in your garden. It will look beautiful planted in a large container, with its soft, tassel-like flower heads having a sculptural appearance during the winter months.

◀LATIN NAME: *Phlomis russeliana*

COMMON NAME: Turkish sage

IDEAL POSITION: Full sun.

CARE: Plant in a well-drained soil and sunny position. Comb and remove any old or dead leaves and flowers in spring.

TIPS: As the seasons change, the yellow flowers turn a deep rust colour. Poking upright from a cloud of evergreen foliage, they make this *phlomis* an excellent year-round plant.

LATIN NAME: *Mahonia eurybracteata* subsp. ▶
ganpinensis 'Soft Caress'

COMMON NAME: **Oregon grape 'Soft Caress'**

IDEAL POSITION: Full sun to shade.

CARE: Feed with plenty of water until established
and during flowering.

TIPS: Plant this specimen shrub in a large
container to elevate its presence. In return it will
prolong a garden's flowering season and attract
wildlife during the winter months.

◀LATIN NAME:
Calamagrostis × acutiflora
'Karl Foerster'

COMMON NAME: **Feather
reed-grass 'Karl Foerster'**

IDEAL POSITION: Full sun to
partial shade.

CARE: Cut down once a
year in late winter before the
new growth appears.

TIPS: The slender green
growth in spring and golden
flower heads in summer will
bring a sense of theatre to
your garden. Keep the dead
flower heads until spring.

◀LATIN NAME:
Veronicastrum virginicum
'Fascination'

COMMON NAME: **Culver's
root 'Fascination'**

IDEAL POSITION: Full sun to
partial shade.

CARE: Divide crowded
clumps in spring.

TIPS: Some prefer to cut
back the plant as its flowers
fade, but if you retain the
dead flower heads, shaped
like fireworks, they will
provide interest through the
winter months.

◀LATIN NAME: *Epimedium ×
perralchicum* 'Fröhnleiten'

COMMON NAME: **Barrenwort
'Fröhnleiten'**

IDEAL POSITION: Full sun to
partial shade.

CARE: This plant needs little
care. It can be easily lifted
and divided in autumn.
If needed, remove dead
leaves in spring.

TIPS: This lovely ground-
cover plant will provide
lasting interest with the ever-
changing colour of its leaves
and bright yellow flowers.

SEASONAL INTEREST

—

◄LATIN NAME: *Lilium regale*

COMMON NAME: **Regal lily; King's lily**

IDEAL POSITION: Full sun.

CARE: Plant bulbs 15–20 cm (6–8 in) deep in soil enriched with well-rotted garden compost. Provide support before the flowers appear in spring. Cut back to ground level in late autumn.

TIPS: Plant in containers near your home for the divine perfume or among other plants for height and grandeur in the garden.

◄LATIN NAME: *Paeonia* 'Buckeye Belle'

COMMON NAME: **Peony 'Buckeye Belle'**

IDEAL POSITION: Full sun to partial shade.

CARE: Remove dead flowers as they fade. Provide slow-release fertilizer around the base of the plant in spring.

TIPS: This peony, with its gorgeous deep red petals and golden stamens, will give your garden a jewel-like appearance in spring.

◄LATIN NAME: *Tropaeolum majus* 'Empress of India'

COMMON NAME: **Nasturtium 'Empress of India'**

IDEAL POSITION: Full sun.

CARE: Remove dead flowers and feed to prolong the flowering season.

TIPS: The orange-ruby flowers will provide interest from early summer well into autumn. Plant in containers for a draping effect or provide support, to create a vertical living sculpture.

◄LATIN NAME: *Fritillaria meleagris*

COMMON NAME: **Snake's head fritillary**

IDEAL POSITION: Full sun to partial shade.

CARE: Plant in fertile, well-drained soil about 10–12 cm (4–5 in) deep in autumn.

TIPS: This plant will never go unnoticed. Flowering in spring, it looks fabulous naturalized in a lawn.

◀LATIN NAME: *Tulipa* 'Spring Green'

COMMON NAME: **Tulip 'Spring Green'**

IDEAL POSITION: Full sun to partial shade.

CARE: To avoid fungal disease, plant bulbs in autumn once the cold weather has set in, in moist, but well-draining soil, in a sunny spot. Does not like water-logged soil.

TIPS: Plant the bulbs in a container and place in the most visible position on the patio.

◀LATIN NAME: *Ammi majus*

COMMON NAME: **Bullwort; Bishop's weed**

IDEAL POSITION: Full sun to partial shade.

CARE: Sow in the ground in autumn for the most flowers and large healthy plants.

TIPS: In groups, it will form large, white clouds above a planting. Scattered, it will bring lightness and height. Flowers continuously for two months from early summer to early autumn.

◀LATIN NAME: *Narcissus* 'Thalia'

COMMON NAME: **Triandrus daffodil 'Thalia'**

IDEAL POSITION: Full sun to partial shade.

CARE: Plant in autumn, 10–15 cm (4–6 in) deep in the ground.

TIPS: This elegant, pure white narcissus makes an excellent plant for spring interest in any type or style of garden, thanks to its timeless, classy appearance. Plant in drifts at the front of a border or in containers visible from indoors.

LATIN NAME: *Iris* 'Superstition'

COMMON NAME: **Bearded iris 'Superstition'**

IDEAL POSITION: Full sun.

CARE: Remove the stems once the flower is over to encourage the formation of new rhizomes.

TIPS: Plant in drifts for a dramatic spring display of rich, deep purple blooms.

LATIN NAME: *Dahlia* 'Verrone's Obsidian'

COMMON NAME: **Dahlia 'Verrone's Obsidian'**

IDEAL POSITION: Full sun.

CARE: Lift and keep in a frost-free position over winter. Provide support while the plant is growing.

TIPS: Use this dahlia to inject your space with a touch of luxuriousness. Sultry, almost black-purple flowers provide interest from mid-summer through to late autumn.

PLANTS FOR
THE KITCHEN

—

◀LATIN NAME: *Allium tuberosum*

COMMON NAME: Chinese chives; garlic chives

IDEAL POSITION: Full sun.

CARE: Keep harvesting to encourage new growth.

TIPS: Plant in containers that can be moved indoors in the winter, to provide a healthy supply of pleasantly sweet, garlic-flavoured leaves all year long.

◀LATIN NAME: *Rosmarinus officinalis*

COMMON NAME: Rosemary

IDEAL POSITION: Full sun.

CARE: Prune in spring and harvest regularly to encourage new growth and stop the plant from becoming leggy and sparse.

TIPS: Grow among ornamental plantings to provide structure and a lovely scent, welcome pollinators and for your culinary enjoyment.

◀LATIN NAME: *Angelica archangelica*

COMMON NAME: Angelica; Angel's fishing rod

IDEAL POSITION: Full sun to partial shade.

CARE: Plant in moist, well-drained soil and don't allow to dry out. It will self-seed if the flower heads are left after turning into seedpods.

TIPS: Will not only look sculptural and beautiful in your garden, but will taste delicious when candied, sautéed or steamed too.

◀LATIN NAME: *Foeniculum vulgare*

COMMON NAME: Fennel

IDEAL POSITION: Full sun.

CARE: Fennel has a tendency to self-seed easily. To keep it in check, remove the yellow flowers before they turn into seedheads.

TIPS: Fennel is not only delicious and widely used in cooking, but it is also an undeniably beautiful plant. Incorporate it into flower borders to create clouds of soft, intricate foliage.

◀LATIN NAME: *Thymus vulgaris*

COMMON NAME: Thyme

IDEAL POSITION: Full sun.

CARE: Harvest regularly to allow for fresh, new growth and to keep the plant from becoming too leggy.

TIPS: This is perhaps one of the most common and popular herbs, and it is grown all around the world. It makes an excellent addition to a herb garden, even if this is located on your balcony.

LATIN NAME: *Fragaria vesca* ▶

COMMON NAME: Wild strawberry

IDEAL POSITION: Full sun to partial shade.

CARE: Plant in a sunny spot and water well and regularly to encourage more fruit. It will thrive in slightly acidic, humus-rich soil.

TIPS: Plant as ground cover to provide seasonal interest and enjoy watching the green carpet of leaves turn white with subtle, fragile flowers, to be replaced later by delicious berries packed with flavour.

LATIN NAME: *Achillea ageratum*

COMMON NAME: English mace; Sweet Nancy; Sweet yarrow

IDEAL POSITION: Full sun.

CARE: Plant in a sunny spot where soil is well draining. Cut right back after flowering for a second, denser clump of foliage.

TIPS: Great in flower arrangements, and its fresh aromatic leaves can be used to season soups, stews, rice and pasta dishes.

LATIN NAME: *Dianthus* 'Mrs Sinkins'

COMMON NAME: Pink 'Mrs Sinkins'

IDEAL POSITION: Full sun.

CARE: Feed with tomato fertilizer and remove dead flower heads to prolong the flowering season. Cut back to ground level once flowering has finished.

TIPS: This is perhaps one of the most glamorous-looking edible plants. Harvest the beautiful white flowers to garnish cocktails.

LATIN NAME: *Centaurea cyanus*

COMMON NAME: Cornflower

IDEAL POSITION: Full sun.

CARE: Deadhead faded blooms to prolong the flowering period. There's no need for fertilizer because, as a wildflower, it will thrive in poor soil.

TIPS: Grow cornflowers not only for their bright blue edible flowers, which have a clove-like taste, but also for their medicinal properties.

LATIN NAME: *Allium ursinum*

COMMON NAME: Wild garlic; Ramson

IDEAL POSITION: Full sun to partial shade.

CARE: Lift and divide large plants into smaller clumps in autumn or spring.

TIPS: Make the most delicious pesto from the leaves and use the beautiful white flowers to season salads, butter, soft cheese or soups.

PLANTS TO CUT

—

◀ LATIN NAME: *Helianthus annuus*

COMMON NAME: **Sunflower**

IDEAL POSITION: Full sun.

CARE: Sunflowers require minimal care and will be happy growing at the back of a border. Collect seeds for next year's harvest.

TIPS: These very affordable and highly successful plants will reward you with spectacular large, honey-coloured flowers that are bound to bring sunshine to any space.

◀ LATIN NAME: *Orlaya grandiflora*

COMMON NAME: **White laceflower**

IDEAL POSITION: Full sun.

CARE: Collect and sow seeds for the following year immediately after the plant has finished flowering.

TIPS: More robust than it first appears, this makes a brilliant cut flower that can last more than a week. Its soft, subtle looks make it perfect for a naturalistic, almost wild bouquet.

◀ LATIN NAME: *Eucalyptus gunnii*

COMMON NAME: **Cider gum**

IDEAL POSITION: Full sun to partial shade.

CARE: Requires minimal pruning if grown as a tree. Otherwise, coppice every two to three years in spring, to maintain at shrub height. This will provide plenty of branches for picking.

TIPS: Consider different types of eucalyptus; there's a wide range of leaf shapes and colour variations.

◀ LATIN NAME: *Echinacea purpurea* 'Virgin'

COMMON NAME: **Purple coneflower 'Virgin'**

IDEAL POSITION: Full sun to partial shade.

CARE: Cut back the stems as the flowers turn pale.

TIPS: This plant will keep producing beautiful white flowers season after season. Its green central cone makes it easy to incorporate into any flower arrangement but it also looks amazing in a bunch on its own.

◀ LATIN NAME: *Echinops ritro* 'Veitch's Blue'

COMMON NAME: **Globe thistle**

IDEAL POSITION: Full sun.

CARE: After the flowers have died, cut the stems right down to the base of the plant to encourage a second flush of flowers.

TIPS: Incredibly popular with bees and insects, this thistle makes an excellent, sculptural cut flower and looks just as good in wintery, dried flower arrangements.

◀ LATIN NAME: *Eryngium giganteum* 'Silver Ghost'

COMMON NAME: **Tall eryngo 'Silver Ghost'**

IDEAL POSITION: Full sun.

CARE: Plant in dry, very well-drained soil. Leave the dead flowers over winter for interest, then lift and divide overcrowded plants in spring.

TIPS: This exceptional, sculptural plant with its spiky silver leaves is perfect for a sophisticated, theatrical flower arrangement.

LATIN NAME: *Verbena bonariensis* ▶

COMMON NAME: **Purple top; Argentinian vervain; South American vervain; Tall verbena**

IDEAL POSITION: Full sun.

CARE: Remove dead stems in spring, when new growth begins to appear.

TIPS: This tall plant, averaging 1.5 m (5 ft) in height, will bring elegance and lightness to your garden, as well as to flower arrangements. Its delicate, purple flowers look brilliant poking out of a tall vase.

167

Plants to Cut

LATIN NAME: *Ridolfia segetum*

COMMON NAME: **False fennel; Goldspray**

IDEAL POSITION: Full sun.

CARE: Pinch out plant tips to encourage bushier growth.

TIPS: Grow false fennel not only for its starburst-like clusters of bright green-gold flowers, which are produced over a long season, but also for its filigree foliage that will add an intricacy and sophistication to your floral arrangements.

LATIN NAME: *Dahlia* 'Café au Lait'

COMMON NAME: **Dahlia 'Café au Lait'**

IDEAL POSITION: Full sun.

CARE: Although dahlias require a lot of care and attention, their flowers are totally worth it. Cut down the stems and carefully lift the tubers as soon as frost starts to blacken the leaves, and allow them to dry naturally indoors before planting the following year after all risk of frost is gone.

When planting, provide enough space between plants to allow them to reach their ultimate height.

TIPS: This extraordinary and extravagant dahlia is a true attention grabber and will make any flower arrangement look luxurious.

LATIN NAME: *Gypsophila paniculata*

COMMON NAME: **Baby's breath**

IDEAL POSITION: Full sun.

CARE: Gypsophila is easy to maintain but doesn't respond well to replanting once established. Plant in groups of three, to develop into bushier, healthy-looking mounds.

TIPS: With its timeless, graceful appearance, gypsophila is an excellent choice for any flower garden, as well as one of the most popular cut flowers for almost any occasion.

PLANTS FOR
WILDLIFE

—

◀LATIN NAME: *Ajuga reptans*

COMMON NAME: **Bugle**

IDEAL POSITION: Full sun or partial shade.

CARE: Divide large clumps in late autumn or early spring, to keep the plant a good shape.

TIPS: Plant bugle, with its short spikes of deep blue flowers, as ground cover, to attract pollinators.

◀LATIN NAME: *Erigeron karvinskianus*

COMMON NAME: **Mexican fleabane**

IDEAL POSITION: Full sun.

CARE: Very easy to look after and grows in the trickiest of soil conditions. Lightly trim any unwanted growth in autumn.

TIPS: Plant Mexican fleabane, with its abundant and long-lasting, delicate, white to pink flowers, to attract bees and butterflies to the garden.

◀LATIN NAME: *Lonicera periclymenum* 'Heaven Scent'

COMMON NAME: **Honeysuckle 'Heaven Scent'**

IDEAL POSITION: Full sun to partial shade.

CARE: If the plant becomes too widespread, cut back the stems by about one-third after it has finished flowering. Apply a generous amount of garden compost around the base of the plant in early spring.

TIPS: The beautifully fragrant flowers of this honeysuckle will attract a variety of wildlife from mid-summer to autumn. It is an excellent plant for pollinators.

LATIN NAME: *Olearia × haastii*

COMMON NAME: **Daisy bush**

IDEAL POSITION: Full sun.

CARE: Remove the flower heads as they fade. Lightly prune in mid- to late spring, to keep the plant to the desired shape.

TIPS: With its abundant and delicate white flowers, greatly loved by pollinators, this makes a brilliant informal hedge for a Mediterranean-inspired garden.

LATIN NAME: *Dipsacus fullonum*

COMMON NAME: **Teasel**

IDEAL POSITION: Full sun or partial shade.

CARE: Collect and propagate by seed in autumn or spring.

TIPS: Teasel is an excellent choice for a wildlife garden, attracting many goldfinches and bees. Leave the dead flower heads, to provide food for birds over winter, or collect them for dry flower arrangements.

LATIN NAME: *Hylotelephium telephium* ▶
(Atropurpureum Group) 'Purple Emperor'

COMMON NAME: Orpine 'Purple Emperor'

IDEAL POSITION: Full sun to partial shade.

CARE: Cut back the old growth and flower
heads from late winter to early spring.

TIPS: 'Purple Emperor' will provide nectar
for butterflies and bees. The flower heads
look wonderful left on the plant over winter,
adding structure, texture and seasonal
interest to a border.

LATIN NAME:
Leucanthemum vulgare

COMMON NAME: Ox-eye
daisy

IDEAL POSITION: Full sun.

CARE: Lift and divide
clumps that have become
too large for their space in
autumn or spring.

TIPS: Deadhead faded
flowers to encourage a
second flush of flowers
later in the season.

LATIN NAME: *Salvia
officinalis* 'Purpurascens'

COMMON NAME: Purple
sage

IDEAL POSITION: Full sun or
partial shade.

CARE: Sage requires little
care and attention. It enjoys
dry weather, so don't over-
water, and only prune lightly
after flowering.

TIPS: Not only is this plant
an excellent choice for
a kitchen garden, it also
has medicinal uses and is
particularly loved by bees.

LATIN NAME: *Agastache*
'Blue Fortune'

COMMON NAME: Giant
hyssop 'Blue Fortune'

IDEAL POSITION: Full sun.

CARE: Lift and divide
clumps that have become
too large for their space in
autumn or spring.

TIPS: The fresh scented
foliage is a magnet for
bees and butterflies.

LATIN NAME: *Aster* ×
frikartii 'Mönch'

COMMON NAME:
Michaelmas daisy

IDEAL POSITION: Full sun.

CARE: Deadhead the faded
flowers to prolong the
flowering period.

TIPS: Asters are incredibly
easy to take cuttings from.
Simply pull away the
rooted sideshoots and
replant directly in the
preferred location.

FEATURED DESIGNERS

—

Unruly Haven, pages 20–5;
City Oasis, pages 112–15
Ula Maria
www.ulamaria.com

Colours of the Desert, pages 26–31
Martha Krempel
www.marthakrempelgardendesign.com

Garden of Contrasts, pages 32–5;
Playing with Shapes and Patterns, pages 116–19
Georgia Lindsay
www.georgialindsaygardendesign.com

City Wildflowers, pages 36–41;
The Power of Simplicity, pages 86–9
Butter Wakefield
www.butterwakefield.co.uk

A Hidden Retreat, pages 42–7;
New Naturalism, pages 52–9;
Clear-cut Minimalism, pages 100–3
Adolfo Harrison
www.adolfoharrison.com

Balcony Garden, pages 48–51
Alice Vincent
Connect with Alice on Instagram @noughticulture

A Touch of the Mediterranean, pages 60–7;
Pared-down Modern, pages 82–5
Miria Harris
www.miriaharris.com

Romantic Idyll, pages 68–73
Phoebe Dickinson
www.phoebedickinson.com

Lavender Hues, pages 74–7
Marlene Fao
www.mymindfulhome.co.uk

Floral Tapestry, pages 78–81
Gabrielle Shay and Silka Rittson-Thomas
www.gabriellegardens.com

Outdoor Room, pages 90–3
Cameron Landscapes & Gardens
www.camerongardens.co.uk

Container Cottage Garden, pages 94–9
Charlie McCormick
www.mccormick.london

Glamorous and Edgy, pages 104–11
Abigail Ahern
www.abigailahern.com

An Enchanting Studio Garden, pages 120–5
The Land Gardeners
www.thelandgardeners.com

Plant Hunter's Dream, pages 126–31
Jack Wallington
www.jackwallington.com

Vintage French, pages 132–7
Gabrielle Shay
www.gabriellegardens.com

MY FAVOURITE SOURCES

———

Here's a list of some of my favourite sources:

LANDSCAPE

All Green Group
www.allgreengroup.co.uk
Stockist of landscaping materials from stone paving and timber to turf and mulch.

Bert & May
www.bertandmay.com
Hand-crafted and reclaimed tiles, plain and patterned, including encaustic cement tiles for outdoor use.

CED Stone
www.cedstone.co.uk
Supplier of natural stone landscaping products, from York stone paving and stone setts to cobbles and pebbles.

The Garden Trellis Company
www.gardentrellis.co.uk
Supplier of trellis panels and wooden fences, gates, arches, arbours, sheds and planters.

London Mosaic
www.londonmosaic.com
Specialists in Victorian floor tiles and contemporary geometric schemes.

Surrey Ironcraft
www.surreyironcraft.com
Made-to-measure architectural metalwork, gates and railings.

Wienerberger
www.wienerberger.co.uk
Bricks, paving, blocks and landscaping materials for outdoor projects.

FURNISH

1stdibs
www.1stdibs.co.uk
Online marketplace and New York store selling original furnishings and treasures from a variety of dealers.

Abigail Ahern
abigailahern.com
Trendsetting product design, including furniture and sculpture, and stockist of faux flowers and plants. As well as garden design, Abigail also runs one-day international Design Masterclasses.

Fermob
www.fermob.com
Manufacturer of garden furniture, from tables and chairs to sun loungers and outdoor sofas, based in France.

Garden Trading
www.gardentrading.co.uk
Practical and stylish garden accessories, lighting, furniture and storage, with a UK showroom based in Oxfordshire.

Hare's Tail Printing
www.harestail.co.uk
Specialist in block printing on vintage sheets and fabrics, which can be made into cushions, hammocks and upholstery.

IKEA
www.ikea.com
A wide range of well-designed, functional home and garden products at affordable prices, flat-packed for home assembly. Stores worldwide.

Jamb
www.jamb.co.uk
Dealer in some of the finest antique and reproduction furniture, with showrooms in the UK and US.

Kadai
www.kadai.co.uk
Specialist in Indian kadai outdoor firebowls, as well as garden planters and décor.

Made.com
www.made.com
Affordable high-end designs, including garden pots and planters, plant stands and garden décor, by emerging designers.

Maisons du Monde
www.maisonsdumonde.com
Wide range of garden furniture, from chairs, tables and sun loungers to cushions, hammocks and parasols, as well as outdoor lighting, ornaments and accessories. Stores worldwide.

Niwaki
www.niwaki.com
Fine pruning tools from Japan, including secateurs (pruning shears), topiary clippers, scissors, shears, loppers, garden saws and sickles.

Raj Tent Club
www.rajtentclub.com
Specialist in decorative Indian tents for sale or rental. Also stocks a complementary range of outdoor sunshades, parasols, furniture, lighting and accessories.

The Shed Builder
www.joelbird.com
Designs and builds made-to-order sheds, outhouses, garden rooms and studios.

Vintage French
www.vintagefrench.com
Web-based dealer specializing in old and antique garden furniture and décor.

WWOO
www.wwoo.nl
Designs multifunctional concrete outdoor kitchens that fit into any garden.

DECORATE

Décors Barbares
www.decorsbarbares.com
Textile design studio of Nathalie Farman-Farma. Her fabrics are inspired by traditional Persian, Asian and Russian costumes, as well as Ballets Russes designs. Showrooms in the UK and US.

Farrow & Ball
www.farrow-ball.com
English paint manufacturer with a palette of timeless colours in a range of exterior finishes. Popular for the sympathetic decorating of historic and traditional properties.

Moonlight Design
www.moonlightdesign.co.uk
Exterior lighting for outdoor landscaping and paths, from solar and underwater lights to wall lanterns and security lights.

PLANT

Crocus
www.crocus.co.uk
A one-stop shop and one of the biggest suppliers of plants in the UK, offering 4,000 varieties, as well as garden tools, outdoor accessories and décor.

David Austin Roses
www.davidaustinroses.co.uk
Award-winning rose breeder, renowned all over the world, and supplier of more than 400 varieties of roses available all year round.

Deepdale
www.deepdale-trees.co.uk
Wide range of bare-root, container and field-grown semi-mature trees, shrubs and instant hedging.

Jekka's
www.jekkas.com
The largest collection of more than 400 culinary and medicinal herb plants in the UK.

Kelways
www.kelways.co.uk
One of the UK's oldest plant nurseries, founded in 1851. Located in Somerset, it offers a wide range of plants, horticultural sundries, pots and planters.

Majestic Trees
www.majestictrees.co.uk
An award winning growers of mature and character trees.

Paramount Plants and Gardens
www.paramountplants.co.uk
The UK's leading specialist for mature trees and shrubs.

Petersham Nurseries
www.petershamnurseries.com
Plant nursery located in Richmond-Upon-Thames that stocks familiar and unusual specimens of plants and flowers alongside artisanal gardening tools and other equipment.

RHS
www.rhs.org.uk
The Royal Horticultural Society is the UK's leading gardening charity.

Sarah Raven
www.sarahraven.com
Popular English gardener, cook, writer and television presenter, Sarah Raven offers a comprehensive range of own-brand seeds, seedlings, plants and gardening and floristry kits.

INDEX

———

INDEX

—

INDEX

ACKNOWLEDGMENTS

Dedicated to Julius, James and Arturas

Thanks to all the wonderful friends, family and colleagues in the gardening world whose support over the years has led me to writing this book. Thanks to every single garden owner and designer for sharing your brilliant gardens that have each inspired me in different ways.

A huge thank you to Jason Ingram, who's captured the beauty of each garden with his genius vision. Thank you to Alison Starling at Octopus for presenting me with this incredible opportunity. I am also very grateful to Art Director Juliette Norsworthy, Managing Editor Sybella Stephens and Production Manager Katherine Hockley for making the book the best it can be.

Last but not least, thanks to my literary agent Zoe King for all of her support along the way.

An Hachette UK Company
www.hachette.co.uk

First published in Great Britain in 2020 by Mitchell Beazley, an imprint of
Octopus Publishing Group Ltd, Carmelite House, 50 Victoria Embankment, London EC4Y 0DZ
www.octopusbooks.co.uk
www.octopusbooks.usa.com

Text copyright © Ula Maria 2020
Photography copyright © Jason Ingram 2020
Design & layout copyright © Octopus Publishing Group 2020

Distributed in the US by Hachette Book Group
1290 Avenue of the Americas, 4th and 5th Floors, New York, NY 10104

Distributed in Canada by Canadian Manda Group
664 Annette Street, Toronto, Ontario, Canada M6S 2C8

ISBN 978 1 78472 601 0

A CIP catalogue record for this book is available from the British Library.
Printed and bound in China

1 3 5 7 9 10 8 6 4 2

Publisher: Alison Starling
Art Director: Juliette Norsworthy
Photographer: Jason Ingram
Senior Managing Editor: Sybella Stephens
Copy Editor: Helen Ridge
Senior Production Manager: Katherine Hockley